FAITH AND DOUBT

Faith and Doubt

by Olivier A. Rabut

TRANSLATED BY BONNIE AND WILLIAM WHITMAN

SHEED AND WARD : NEW YORK

© *Sheed and Ward, Inc., 1967*

This book first appeared in 1964, under the title
La Vérification Religieuse, *published by Les
Editions du Cerf, Paris.*

Nihil obstat:
>*Brendan W. Lawlor*
>*Censor Librorum*

Imprimatur:
>✠ *Robert F. Joyce*
>*Bishop of Burlington*
>*September 6, 1967*

*The Nihil Obstat and Imprimatur are official dec-
larations that a book or pamphlet is considered to
be free of doctrinal or moral error. No implication
is contained therein that those who have granted
the Nihil Obstat and Imprimatur agree with the
contents, opinions, or statements expressed.*

Library of Congress Catalog Card Number 67-29288

Manufactured in the United States of America

CONTENTS

CONTENTS

FAITH AND DOUBT

Let them rage against you, those who have no inkling of the blood and tears that even the slightest knowledge of the true God demands. Let them be incensed with you, those who have never been turned aside, as you and I have. As for me, I would find it utterly impossible to be angry with you . . .

But I must ask you a favor, so that you should not be angry with me in turn . . . . Let us, you and I, lay aside all arrogance. Let neither of us pretend to have found the truth. Let us seek it as something unknown to both of us. Then we may seek it with love and sincerity, when neither of us has the rashness or presumption to believe that he already possesses it. And if I am asking too much of you, allow me to listen to you at least, to talk with you as I do with beings whom, for my part, I do not pretend to understand.

—ST. AUGUSTINE, *Contra Epistolam Manichaei,* CH. 3.

Introduction
The Desire for Verification

TODAY MUCH is known about the spiritual problems that trouble twentieth-century man. Catholics recognize that these problems can no longer be avoided or even feared. It is better to look them squarely in the face, realizing that they will require us to analyze and reconstruct our current thinking in a thorough manner. Either we admit that urgency, or we ignore the present-day situation. True, without the necessary spiritual and intellectual training, many people would find this a dangerous enterprise. However, it is essential that there are a few who undertake a thorough study of the problems, dedicating their lives to this task; otherwise, the Church will fail in one of its *vital functions*.

What function? It has often been said that the *Christian world* and the *modern world* are no longer attuned to one another; they share neither the same cultural heritage, nor the same tastes, nor the same needs. They not only have trouble understanding one another; they are hardly able to focus on the same question. They differ somewhat in their basic inquiry, their basic enterprise. Two sound attitudes are possible in this situation; but one, I feel, is far better than the other.

The first is very prevalent and means an adaptation of the self, a willingness "to conform," to speak and dress like others as much as possible. Through caution or lack of courage, one holds back from any profound transformation of the self, for one does not feel ready for a thorough recasting. One is in danger of only *appearing* to be modern, and this is fruitless and harmful.

The second attitude is far more costly and risky. It examines the intellectual needs that structure the modern world, does not reject their radical nature, and accepts them to the degree that they can be sanctioned. The Christian does not dream up expedients but makes modern research his own. He tries to grasp its meaning, he joins in with it in its fundamental thrust and aim; he applies it to the questions closest to his heart—religious questions.

Let us take a simple example. In today's world it is no longer uncommon for a theologian to be schooled in the sciences. He profits from it considerably; he throws off cramping influences, as it were, for his outlook broadens; he gains a sound understanding of the material universe and the temporal functions of man. He enters into fruitful exchanges with his contemporaries. But his participation in the sciences introduces him to a new need, one which may still be somewhat unclear in his mind. Will he apply it to his theology and, on a deeper level, to his decision to believe?

Today's research, if we do not limit its scope, requires us to justify our faith in precise terms. This should be done through a fresh approach, without haste (and certainly not by the methods of science but by those appropriate to the endeavor). If we are to deal with the current spiritual problem at its roots, we must, some of us at least, make the necessary effort. Let us be warned that this is a formidable task.

"The modern world" is clearly a reality. It has been taking shape for several centuries, and is now in the process of solidifying. The positions it is adopting are very forceful, disquieting perhaps and false in places, but nevertheless solid, even uncompromising, and often very intelligent.

The attentive observer's first discovery—or better, first surprise—is that a convergence is taking place: diverse elements are being gathered into a single current; tentative methods and casts of mind strike a note of resonance and are mutually strengthened; the transformation is unifying; the new spirit has strong advantages at its disposal, and great resources.

The second surprise is that the research animating this new spirit is basically compatible with the Gospel. It is a part of what Christians themselves should have developed, especially the fervent concern for truth, the stubborn resolution to probe religious questions until answers are found, the refusal to be satisfied with a naïve and predefined faith, the determination to discuss the problem with all the depth and thoroughness one can bring to bear. This rigorous approach is consistent with the evangelic inspiration.

After an initial delay, Catholic exegesis awoke to this fact before it was too late. But the question is deeper than and goes beyond exegesis. It concerns suppositions which the exegete, the theologian, or the apologist instinctively takes as his own. The discussion revolves around the methods, the hidden options, the spirit of the research. What are the steps which begin in darkness and emerge into the light, allowing us to determine that a given thing merits belief? This is one of the shafts we must sink, to strengthen the foundations of our faith.

Christianity must answer for the soundness of the positions it upholds; this is one of its tasks. But the unbeliever seeks to do this too. Are the two efforts identical? The important point here is that each party has its own way of looking at the process. I believe that this area is one where an understanding is possible (provided certain serious obstacles can be overcome). Both parties will agree, I hope, that each has a role to play.

If many of our contemporaries are in partial or total doubt with respect to the dogmas, it is often because they cannot do otherwise *in good conscience*. Every act should be capable of justification, particularly the act of believing. A person who has been completely honest in his religious thought and who, in light of his present convictions, simply does not see a way to believe would have no right to endorse the assertions of the Church.[1]

But why should this man be estranged from religious aims? If he doubts through integrity, then an intense religious life is possible. He wants to go the entire distance in his search for truth. If he feels that Christianity does not oppose the process whereby one demonstrates the soundness of one's assertions, he could share in many of the spiritual riches of the Gospel. From Abraham's time on, the Christian movement has possessed these vital riches; it would be foolish to ignore them, even if one feels that the customary way they are presented should be revised. Who could look at the Himalayas and declare that the view is banal?

An admirer, however, is not necessarily one who is convinced. He may stick to his reservations. He should not be asked to believe. This would not only mean hoping for the impossible, but in the cases I have in mind, it might also mean forcing the person toward a premature decision—a spiritually dangerous step. For many years the vocation of such a person will be to fail to see the truth. He would not be in earnest if he were too quick to embrace a doctrine that did not answer to his soul.

It is obvious that Christ does not reject such men—on the

contrary, he came for them—and the sincere doubter does not reject Christ. Nietzsche saw this point clearly; phrases such as "the Christian conscience quickened in the confessionals" and "intellectual purity desired at any price" are critical remarks which do Christianity credit. The concept of total surrender to truth, the taste for purity developed in us by an ancient Christian heritage, have raised a vital question. Is belief necessary? Often twentieth-century man has no answer. Therefore, let him live in doubt, but as a lover of truth and spiritual perfection. His thirst is so great that he cannot refuse the wine, though he may question the vintage on the label.

Doubt and religious indifference are very different attitudes. The uncertainty we are considering here is antithetical to indifference. The great evil today, as always, is that most people *are not interested* in spiritual values.[2] The inquirer we have in mind, however, feels that a vital current flows through Christianity, and he makes the effort necessary to participate in it. He nonetheless exercises a deliberate doubt, one whose scope he carefully defines.[3] We are going to study the conditions which allow doubt to be compatible with the faith that delivers and illuminates; in fact, this will be our primary aim. Our method will be to express doubts, strongly and systematically.

Those who have experienced Christianity know that it has a simple majesty, a modest and very sound center. It cannot be reached by rational argument, for it is located on another level. We must try to gain an inner understanding of this fact. We are speaking here of a special way of life that *listens* to reality—all reality—and receives a kind of *living knowledge* of its secret laws. We will try, then, to focus on Christianity's virtues, to be receptive to its spiritual impulse.

This aim cannot be incompatible with the terrible need for truth that some men harbor within. But there is a hidden spark in the lives of really religious men, a spark which in itself constitutes a truth. We would like to make contact with this particular phenomenon—to handle it, to examine it, to experience it in a spirit of honesty and respect. We will avoid theoretical discussions (which have their place elsewhere) in order to classify these questions; moreover, controversy would obscure the hidden light whose presence we propose to study.

The difficulty lies in delving through the mountain of debris that hides the real Christianity, so that we can perceive its true greatness. Every man should succeed in this quite well, provided he accepts the fact that he will not see clearly on the first try. A long series of steps, patiently taken, is necessary before he will reach the heart of Christianity, before he can partake of the vital knowledge which will allow him to distinguish the heart from everything surrounding it.

Introduction: The Desire for Verification

NOTES

1. If this surprises some Catholics, they should refer to St. Thomas, who does not hesitate to say, "It is immoral to believe in Christ if one's reason does not condone one's doing so. Everyone should obey his conscience, even if it leads him into error" (I. II. 19, 5). Of course, the error of conscience should not be deliberate, as would be the case if it were committed through carelessness (*ibid*. a. 6).

See Acts 17, 11, for one's right and at times one's duty not to believe until one has demonstrated the soundness of one's beliefs: "These were more noble than those in Thessalonica, in that they received the word with all readiness of mind, and searched the scriptures daily, whether those things were so." (The problem today implies that faith in the Scriptures must also be justified.)

2. See again Acts 17, 11.

3. Deliberate doubt, we will see further on, differs profoundly from Descartes' methodical doubt. We do not mean that beliefs whose soundness has not been established must be eradicated from the mind. The intellect normally makes use of a strong foundation of predefined elements; it is sufficient to make a distinction between that which has been critically established and that which has not.

Moreover, we will see that there is a well-established and possibly ineffable fact whose consequences are not well determined but whose possession assures the richness and equilibrium of spiritual life and religious knowledge. This fact removes doubt to a less important level. This fundamental idea will be developed in the course of our study.

I
Initial Considerations

1. ELEMENTARY
RELIGIOUS PERCEPTIONS

PRIOR TO ANY ELABORATION of doctrine, religious knowledge is to be found in several initial perceptions—parent-intuitions which are the source of later definitions and of any subsequent debate. These great initial perceptions require a well-defined attitude toward life, and people whose lives are badly oriented will find them almost impossible to attain. Consequently, we must proceed through a series of approximations, improving our lives step by step as we gain an increasing awareness of fundamental realities. Although we can never make them fully our own, we must be in constant search of them, and this in itself implies that we have already glimpsed them.

Our study will begin on the level of these elementary perceptions. Should it seem too vague, we answer that although we too like precision, we feel that an examination should begin with the trunk, not the branches. Our experience has convinced us that one should be thoroughly acquainted with these fundamental perceptions for the sake of spiritual life and intellectual speculation. They are the form, the whole in which the particulars find their place. In and of themselves they do not remove the problems, but they help us to see them in proper perspective; and we need not wait for ultimate solutions in order to live with truth.

We are only too familiar with a conventional and extremely verbalized religion, one which is unreal despite the seriousness surrounding it; in fact, this very seriousness often makes it forced and artificial. For many of us, all that has long since been discarded. And many have experienced a sort of liberation; after finding themselves completely naked and defenseless in front of life, doubting everything, blindly participating in humanity's lot and its everyday activities, they arrive at a certain clarity of vision. Having achieved this state, they can undertake their apprenticeship in religious life.

Let us return to the roots; let us patiently strive to restore modesty and value. In due time we will witness a gradual renovation; a new life will blossom forth, a new constellation will form. All the old ideas will appear in a new form, each one transfigured. Yet the new vision will reintegrate the sound elements of the old and may show exactly what the old was attempting to express. There is a marked difference between the two—a pile of planks does not resemble a growing tree. But the new vision is not yet a tree; it is only fertile ground, only a start, with all the simplicity and limitations of a beginning.

A monk once suggested that one meditate on the attributes of God by devoting one day to concentrating on his total power, the next on his benevolence, and so on in this manner. But today many people feel that God has no known or definable qualities. We have yet to learn how to welcome all events and to open ourselves to our human brothers, how to cling with a sort of love to the destiny that has been given to us—so that if there is anything noble and good to be had from reality, we will receive it with open hearts. I am reminded of a great philosopher, an unbeliever, who attended Holy Week services. He was attentive to all that took place, anxious to receive everything there was to be had.

If there is something that can be called Transcendence, if there is a divine current running through our lives, we must welcome it peacefully and respectfully. The name that we give to this sort of experience is relatively unimportant, but if there is a Holy Spirit (whatever the exact meaning of this term may be), it is essential that we make contact with it. A current is flowing, and we must allow ourselves to be carried by it. There is a pulse beating here; on the surface its existence could be questioned, but if one could discover its hidden axis, it would no doubt prove to be invaluable.

In this spirit it is possible to see the great Christian themes in their extreme simplicity: the happiness of being righteous, first celebrated in the Gospel of Luke; the value of a deep understanding of other men; the value of sympathy, good faith, and forgiveness; the blessedness of a soul large enough to transcend petty calculations—"whosoever shall compel thee to go a mile, go with him twain"—a soul that finally receives total illumination—"if thine eye be single, thy whole body shall be full of light."

These and other themes are often obscured by the zealous efforts of scholastics bent upon establishing an elaborate doctrine. They also suffer when drawn into simplistic syntheses of thought. If we identify sin with violations of a moral code, we are distorting the teaching of the Gospel. If we identify good with a particular group—for example, the Church, as a body with limited membership—we are in danger of embracing the very antithesis of Christianity.

Let us take a closer look at the main theme of Christianity: salvation. We can build on rock or on sand. Man is always subject to self-degradation, to total waste of his being; yet there are people who deepen their lives, discover their harmony with all reality, attune themselves to the fount of being. Just as a dislocated shoulder can be set, certain beings will realize the dreadful abyss to be avoided. A sort of ascensional force begins to work within them, their water is changed to wine, and the old man is replaced by the new.

We are speaking here of an immediate salvation, whatever its extension after death may be. A doubter might find some experiential evidence for the existence of an afterlife by looking to those men who have opened themselves to Christianity sufficiently to be transformed. Are such men rare? Most Christians subscribe to the Gospel mentally, but do not

dare to live by it. On the other hand, many people do go beyond the stage of idle impulse and make an honest attempt
to follow Christ; but they are less in evidence, and the fruits
of their efforts are little known. Simple beings can experience renewed life and inner purification, yet remain in the
realm of human imperfection. Comparable simplicity is also
found in people of great intelligence. We admire a young
mother's cheerfulness, her equilibrium, clear-sightedness,
and imperturbable serenity. Thirty years later we find that
the promise has been kept—her vigor has not been spent.
The parish church in small towns is constantly producing
results of this kind.

A person considering such facts will certainly concede
their validity; reservations he still may have will involve
secondary matters. Anyone who can open himself to Christianity's current will find his central self improved, though
perhaps not his peripheral self. If we study the lives of those
who answer Christianity's call with a total commitment, we
can see the true picture of its power to save. This means an
unstinting effort to open oneself to it and to be transformed.

Admittedly this is a very difficult thing to do. We are
afraid to turn ourselves over completely to the ecclesiastical
mechanism. And rightly so, when this means that we lose
our critical faculty and our freedom of judgment, when we
allow ourselves to fall under the influence of a group that
holds controvertible ideas—a group skillful at imposing its
practices, its culture, and even its political concepts. By doing

this we would be naïvely exposing ourselves to a *religious* reality and, at the same time and in spite of ourselves, would be sinking into a *human* frame of reference that denies us our freedom, our brotherhood with the modern world, our taste for a new civilization, and our search for a true science and a true philosophy. This is a very real danger; but in this study (and in further writings) we hope to show that it can be avoided. It is indispensable that we keep ourselves above questionable human influences, just as it is indispensable that we find our honey, our religious sustenance, there where it is to be found.[1]

At some time, then, we must take the first step toward our conversion. This is an act of turning about; we turn toward a reality that transforms life. As we stand by this act, seeking to intensify it, we are not compromising the possibility of a straightforward discussion. But if we do not manage to perceive the germ of fertility, no movement will have been started and fruitful discussion will be impossible. True perception already means adherence to the kernel of excellence in Christianity, but it does not necessarily represent uncritical endorsement of the details of Christian doctrine and discipline. To begin with, then, we must *appreciate what is good* and move forward to meet it.

A conversion cannot be justified or explained by means of reason—for the discovery of this "new world" is

neither effected *in* reason nor even *through* reason. For
there is the discovery, a direct and almost immediate
experience (immediate psychologically, not in the sense
of time). Then reason comes on the scene, doing its best
to give reasons for this turning about which it does not
understand. And one always finds reasons—I myself
could give any number. But they are of secondary importance, and inferior by nature. If a convert considers
them of prime importance, then it seems to me his conversion is incomplete. Since this is unfortunately often
the case, many conversions are nothing but a blind alley.
In general, priests too are making reason a means to
justify faith, and this is why there will be no more
entries into the Church. This is a pity, for a great many,
too many, will never discover the Source.

Can a fish that has left the water explain to another
fish what it rediscovers about water on its return?[2]

Obviously reason does have a place in this matter; and as
the faculty that discerns, it may have a difficult role to play.
But it must be perceptive enough to begin with the essential
and to recognize a new reality which must be tested and
savored. We could not respect a doctor who did not bother
with the practical aspects of his work, saying that his understanding was still incomplete and that his theory was not
ready. Here the decisive experience is a vital movement

which opens us to the religious action of Christ and the Church, enabling us to confirm it as sound and good.

Therefore, we must understand what is meant by the promise of Christ:

> If any man thirst, let him come unto me, and drink. He that believeth on me, as the scripture hath said, out of his belly shall flow rivers of living water. (John 7, 37–38)

What is meant by the living water? What is the deliverance proclaimed to us here? Science, art, and human culture all offer man a certain salvation and deliverance; yet evidently something else is intended—although temporal salvation does stem somehow from religious salvation.

Or again, let us reflect upon the proclamations of the Book of Isaiah (55, 1–2):

> Ho, every one that thirsteth, come ye to the waters, and he that hath no money, come ye, buy, and eat; yea, come, buy wine and milk without money and without price. Wherefore do ye spend money for that which is not bread? and your labor for that which satisfieth not? Hearken diligently unto me, and eat ye that which is good, and let your soul delight itself in fatness.

Let us look to good things, to substantial foods, and try to discern which of them are truly religious. They constitute a special group, one for which we must acquire the taste and the understanding.

NOTES

1. The meaning we give to the words "religious" and "religion" will become clearer in the following pages. But we must clear up an initial ambiguity that may exist. To some, these words suggest a special function outside of human life as seen in its ultimate meaning. A life can be more or less religious, whether or not it contains doubt; if there were no element of doubt, there would be no ultimate meaning within man's reach.

What is this final significance, this ultimate dimension, of life? The theologian defines it as a relationship to God as established through the free act. (Any act carried out with some element of freedom says "yes" or "no" to God, whether we are aware of this or not.) Starting with this premise and making no assumptions, we will make personal contact with the religious character of a life, instead of trying to define it. Obviously this means contact with that which is sacred, whatever reality this word finally designates.

2. An anonymous testimony in *J'ai rencontrè le Dieu vivant* (Témoignages: *Revue des Jeunes*).

2. BEYOND THE TEMPORAL

THE PARTICULAR REALITY with which we must make contact appears in everyday life and is, in a sense, always close at hand. But although it is merged in the temporal, it surpasses the temporal in nature. By the word *temporal* ("that which happens in time") we mean the entire output of a civilization, including its intellectual fruits such as science and literature. What does this definition imply? The answer will come to light in the course of our study.

A civilization may reach eternal values through works such as art and philosophy, but it can only do so sporadically. More frequently it is love and devotion in everyday life that kindles the new quality which is capable of reaching the threshold we have in mind. We must go further and add that it is essential to recognize at the beginning that the works of civilization, however ingenious and refined, are only indications of what we must pass beyond in order to find the religious spark. It is not found in them, but is of another order.

We think it would be helpful to illustrate this by discussing a number of experiences where temporal circumstances play a significant role. Hopefully this will serve to show up the reality which lies beyond. Certain experiences may cause a person to emerge a new man. His eyes are opened, he finally comes to understand two or three simple and essential facts. And although his discoveries may cost him a great deal, they are so important that he has no regrets.

War or deportation could illustrate our theme, as could, perhaps, the proletarian condition. Without doubt, love or failure in any form could—provided the experience is a profound one. But let us restrict ourselves to an everyday occurrence: disease.

UNBEARABLE SUFFERING

We do not realize how much suffering the body can cause us, still less the shock that suffering produces on the soul. It comes as a cruel awakening—that reality contains this! A person in acute pain cries out, and his cry is an expression of indignant surprise. He assumed that the world had at least a minimum of order and stability, and now he is bitterly disillusioned. Suddenly a breach appears, one which has been concealed and which seems to affect the whole of reality and the ultimate foundations of being. To see it is to experience supreme disillusionment. Am I nothing but chaos? Is the totality of the real nothing but inanity?

We fall prey to a disorder, sinking deeper and deeper into its clutches; we may endure it, or we may die from it. It raises certain thought-provoking but futile questions. Is it admissible that a human being suffer so? If a man inflicted this sort of suffering on himself or on another, he would be a criminal. Can any sin justify so much suffering? But the parable of the man born blind teaches us that the affliction is not a punishment for our transgressions.

The abyss of physical suffering evokes other griefs: sickness, madness, inborn perversity, degradations that kill all human dignity. In fact, there is a similarity and a convergence in all of them. The abyss is always the same; only the paths leading to it differ. Must we conclude that reality is utterly absurd? Does God abandon a part of his creation to darkness?

The tortured man experiences a questioning that orients his whole being, inclining him toward an extremely dangerous spiritual attitude. For his reason if not for his life— and for his Christian fidelity, in any case—it is important at the time of crisis that he open himself to another vital orientation. He must admit, hypothetically at least, that his problem is not insoluble. Perhaps this absurdity is not irreducible,

35

despite appearances to the contrary. An inner voice, one which he can either heed or stifle at its source, awakens and tells him that perhaps this is good in spite of everything. At moments of complete helplessness, when all free action seems impossible, when he seems completely overcome by weakness and chaos, he still has the choice of accepting or rejecting this voice. "And what if it is good that I suffer so?"

The possibility is there. It does not have to mean resignation. The crisis causes him to question all preconceived positions, and if he should retain a former conviction, he must totally re-create it with a thoroughness and discrimination he would formerly have found inconceivable.

If we failed to call evil by its name, we would be committing a sort of crime against truth and human prerogatives. Revolt is a proof of greatness, but it should be confined to areas to which it is suited. We are tempted to make a total and final revolt. It is difficult to find a place for what is beyond evil and beyond revolt, difficult not to exclude a hidden higher harmony worthy of our allegiance. There is only one possible answer: wherever evil abounds, a grace or meaning superabounds. We can no longer conceive of a grace that allows so much havoc, but neither can we honestly conceive of any real fact that precludes the possibility of its existence.

It is remarkable that we find traces of similar perturbations in the Bible. It is all there, wherever one looks for it. We can encounter it especially in the Psalms, and it is expressed most dramatically in Job. The pious man should abandon the explanations he used to cite to other people, for a crucial moment comes when they prove illusory. When the unhappy man finds himself in the throes of a transformation, he may not be the master of his thoughts and feelings, but he is still the master of his fidelity in the essential part of his movement toward God. As he takes his stand beyond all reasoning and images, as he denounces the theories he has been taught—even prior to finding a better one to take their place—he preserves the integrity of a kernel of faith and hope that he himself cannot define. By this alone is he saved.

ANTICIPATION OF DEATH

A person who is seriously ill sometimes feels that he is letting go of the vital cord that holds his organism together, as if the stones of the house were slightly loosening without quite breaking apart. Now it is no longer a question of pain itself, though pain does add to this feeling. The patient enters a world whose boundaries are novel sensations totally unfamiliar to healthy people. The simplest of these might be described as feverishness, nausea, chills, exhaustion; yet these terms are only approximate. There is a sensation which goes beyond the particular symptoms of the illness, a sordid impression that the organism is a swamp of pestilence, one corruption following another. The patient feels a breaking up of that convergence of elements whose vigor constitutes life.

To say that such an impression is painful is beside the point. It is actually a warning, a sort of test where several essential aspects of the human condition make themselves felt. For want of stronger terms,[1] we might say that weakness and loneliness emerge first. Then comes a realization of the tendency to live with illusions. The purpose of life is partially unveiled, at least in a negative way. The patient realizes his mistake in yielding to the attractions of pleasure, knowledge, social action, art, or even apostleship (here we do not contest the idea that these pursuits, in themselves, may be necessary). He catches a glimpse of an altogether different goal, the true one and finally the only one; he must keep watch for it, wait for it—and not give it a name too quickly.

As the symptoms develop, even those people who love the patient cannot really know what is taking place. He is ill; he is changing color. What is happening to him? The essential is incommunicable. And this is just as well, for there are questions which each person must solve for himself. Moreover, what is taking place is a personal matter between him and God; there has been a silent conversation, and a third party cannot understand it.

The lesson here is that the final word on one's life is not knowable to the world and to men. One dies alone facing God—this is a certainty, and we must all prepare ourselves for it. Once this ordeal clarifies our human existence, then everything that is not a part of this ultimate facing of God is reduced to a state of contingence.[2]

The person who is gravely ill does not choose his acute loneliness. He wants to return to the world, to happiness, but this time to try to embrace them in their true meaning.

We should not put things behind us, but should look to them for true communion with the Father. We will founder, missing the meaning of life, unless we determine life's real connection with God. Not the mental connection, for one can think of God and forget the world in a way that merely adds to one's store of illusions. Many are the vocations, but the basic law is always the same: one may participate in the world or retire from it, but the value of one's life stems from the trueness of one's connection to God.

No doubt our Western minds are too accustomed to certain strict thought-patterns to allow us to see an experience of grave illness for what it is. How would I express it if I did not believe in God? It would be wholly unfitting to take such a naked, rough, elementary, and holy encounter, to consider its usefulness for apologetic ends, and to utilize it in the support of certain preestablished views. We are touching the rock here. Whatever certainty we now have must not be compromised by a preconceived interpretation. In the barometric emptiness of the goods of this world, we must hold to our belief that the human being and his inner action have meaning; we must realize that our individual positions with regard to suffering, death, and life really matter. The ordinary concerns of men seem trivial, but we can attain a simple inner nobility, a truth, an eternal quality in our actions. It is of utmost importance to step forth into pure air.[3] We realize that man's destiny is to give his life value and meaning. The world may disappear, but there is still an incontestable ideal worthy of all heroic acts.

The ultimate meaning of human life (and it does have meaning—we are approaching it) is not found in our association with the world but in our contact with a mysterious term which we might call the Holy, or the Foundation, or the All, or the Transcendence. Experience does not equip us to say the least thing about the nature of this term, nor does it demonstrate the existence of God. But meaning, which is rectitude or truth, means contact with this term which is neither world nor man. Defining it is of no great importance. And although there is the chance that the concept of God that we inwardly hold may be faulty, it is better to represent the Transcendence inadequately than to underestimate the value of our structural relationship to it. Finally,

experience shows that conceptual explanations count for
little if the act is worthy.[4]

THE HUMAN CONDITION

A person who has formed the habit of exercising his
spiritual powers knows that they function independently of
his bodily states. He says to himself that his soul will continue along its path regardless of what happens to his body;
he loves God and he is living as he should. It is a good thing
when one reaches this point, when one attains that stability
in which the spirit is fixed on its proper pole and is little
concerned with physical states; while the spirit may be
bothered at times, it is not brought to a standstill, for it exercises a certain control which overrides pain.

This supposes that we are built with a certain threshold
of physical energy and balance. If the health of the organism
sinks below that threshold, one's mastery disappears. A person retains his desire for the good, but his perception is
troubled and his will weakens. He begins to question the
principles he has been living by; his foundations totter. This
marks a turning point. He faces the possibility of enormous
growth, or disaster. It is a singular occasion, an opportunity

to throw off old prejudices and to delve deeper into the reasoning behind his basic commitments. This could mean a breakthrough, a recasting of the foundations of his being. But he is also tempted to shuck off everything and to put nothing in its place. His foundations may already be somewhat provisional and presumptive by nature; and letting them go, he may find it easier not to try to replace them with something better. As he faces this marvelous opportunity to gain lucidity, objectivity, and sound choice, he also runs the risk of dispersing his earlier spiritual attainments.

A person who considers himself sound may harbor the same weakness. Clearly, extinction of the active powers of the soul through bodily decay is an accident and an exception. Unusual is the case when a given mechanism manifests and accentuates an underlying weakness. In everyday life the weakness lies hidden in a veil of illusions. But there is only a superficial difference between an accident of this kind and the cases thought of as sound. Rarely does the intellect see with candor and clarity; rarely is the will in command. We are almost always pursuing a temptation that has gotten a hold on us.[5]

If we were to select the particular temptation that will dominate us, the evil would be limited in scope; all too often, however, chance makes this selection for us. And consistent domination by a single temptation creates an impression of stability. But a slight organic or mental change—particularly if it jells—a period of indolence, a shift of focus, the appearance of a new temptation, and man betrays what he holds dearest. Psychologists know how powerful our instinctive motivations are. Instinct is a good thing, but difficult to use and control—in most cases it stifles freedom. All that we are saying here is applicable to men of standing, the famous and the admired, as well as to "ordinary" men.

Nevertheless, occasionally a spark of the spirit is successful. Human existence is poised on this paradox: the greatest of stakes—the spirit's possibilities—are intrinsically bound to a house of cards. Strictly mediocre qualities dwell within us, in close association with divine qualities, the former often ensnaring the latter. Should this cause us to despair? No, it is better to rejoice over the openings in the sky offered to us by this block of matter. But we must be well aware of our congenital weakness and of the deep implications of the experiences we have just examined.

We could cite other cases, many more than one would think. Often all that man has left to offer God is his suffering. All the saints, regardless of whether they entered the special avenues open to mystics, encountered this important law governing spiritual life: our security does not reside within us, but in God's mercy, in our maintaining a deep contact with the Father.

Other men, those who have had no involvement with theology, have found that suffering, failure, sin, and even joy give them an understanding of their frailty as well as of the grandeur the human being is sometimes granted. There is an element worthy of respect in those who suffer, and even in those who sin, when a certain real intensity is reached; the great laws of the human condition are manifesting themselves through these people. The painter Munch said, "I want to represent beings that breathe, feel, love and suffer. The spectator should recognize what is sacred in them, so that he will discover himself in them, as in the church."[6]

An excessively rational way of conceiving of things leads us to the point where everything collapses and a valuable life can finally rise out of the ruins. Often the instinctive defenses a creature uses to oppose the work of God are broken down by an emotionally shattering experience. And, then, something entirely new begins in the darkness.

We must try to reflect, now that we have been warned by the accounts of these experiences. They bring us to a realization, actually a quite simple one, but one which each of us must ultimately come to of himself—though most of us do not achieve it in a complete manner. It is not enough to quote Pascal's observations on straying from the path, not enough to read a book or to sermonize to oneself. The question is, What do we need? And the answer must come from our innermost selves—an answer derived from our own experience.

Beyond the Temporal

We want comfort, health, a sound culture, a good social structure, courage, justice. But is this enough? Without turning away from these goals, but rather in order to invest them with an absolute value, man seeks to model himself on a higher plan. Plato said, "a man should honor his soul" and "a man must escape toward the divine." Buddhism tells us that we must start with the search for the *self*—all else is vanity. Saint-Exupéry maintained that "there is a part of man more worthy of saving than happiness." Aldous Huxley declared that time will run out, that is, that there is an urgent necessity to seek abiding values.

But what we have seen up to this point is inconclusive, and has been set forth in a largely negative way: *we seek a richness which is not to be found in temporal goals.* To express this in a positive way, and for lack of a better term, we use the word "eternal" to designate the particular quality of those values that transcend time. This expression calls for explication, lest it appear ambiguous.

"Eternal" does not mean infinite duration; once we understand that the nontemporal goals really exist, personal immortality is still an open question. It would also be a mistake to deprecate man in his normal round of affairs by showing that he lacks orientation in the higher spheres. We cannot attain the eternal without making a thorough study of the concrete. "Eternal" does not mean time—even infinite time —though it is not found outside time. When we interpret Plato's concept of "escape toward the divine," we certainly admit the idea of an ascension toward transcendental values, but we do not subscribe to an escape that implies an abandoning of the earth—the place of our duties.

The eternal is not an "abstract" part of man, with no individual or historical function, but is, on the contrary, what is most concrete in man: *the ultimate meaning of the historical and the personal,* the absolute meaning of what is most personal within us. Clearly it is not the superficial, the peripheric, the illusory states of the *I*. It is, rather, the depth, the nonusable, that which, once realized, has a definitive range. When the act is performed, its meaning abides (St. Francis Assisi leaving the paternal house) in all its complexity, harboring controvertible elements as well as a value that triumphs over time.

NOTES

1. Probably music and poetry come closest to expressing this. Especially Rilke, *The Book of Poverty and Death.*

2. The expression "facing God" is open to debate. God is never in front of us, never subject to *confrontation*—rather, he encompasses us. The phrase used here is meant to evoke man's constituent relationship to God and the orientation toward God necessary for the authenticity of life.

3. An example of this kind is found in *Journal d'un condamné à mort,*

published by the *Revue de Paris*, March 1947. The author, who was facing imminent death over a long period of time, came to feel that the only things of value were true love, friendship in the deepest sense, mystical inquiry, and perhaps art. We would say that art should certainly be included if it proceeds from the need for absolute authenticity.

4. These explanations take on a vital importance later on, in that they embody the fruit of research and devotion to truth.

Thus, we might wonder whether the human being does not create the meaning which he attributes to himself and to things. Would I not be the unconscious author of a subjective interpretation if I felt, after a period of suffering, that I had established the real meaning of human life? But I recognize that my life has meaning apart from my suffering—meaning which I do not choose and which I may not be conscious of. There is an obvious purpose in life, which is probably one of the most pure that man can hope for. Fundamental human dynamism is grasped outside of contingent variations and its artificial adjuncts. The meaning of human reality is imposed upon us; man can only perceive it in this way. The human being's destiny includes more than the world, that is, it loses its value if it does not make contact with another end. This is the only true interpretation for man. As man cannot extricate himself from the interpretations he is wont to make, the meaning he sees is ultimate, the true one in our field of perspective. It expresses reality in the only way that man can interpret it. In strict terms, this is all that is necessary. We believe that one should go further and conclude that the human intellect can also discover the meanings inscribed in the real, although, in ascertaining them, the intellect reconstructs them to a certain extent; this could be backed up by arguments of greater scope and by research which would take us into metaphysics itself.

5. On this point, see Carrouges, *De T. E. Lawrence à Boukarine* (The Power of Fascination), in *La Vie Intellectuelle,* August-September 1949, p. 163:

"At the source of our actions, especially the actions essential to our destiny, there is something incredibly enigmatic which in the main escapes the intellect. And this is even truer of the forces behind language and memory.

"An incomprehensible power of fascination acts upon us, at the heart of the psychic forces formed by our interests, our desires, the words that make an impression on us, the images that inspire us, and the actions and situations that bewilder us."

6. From Munch's *Journal,* 1889.

3. THE NEW FIRE

PEOPLE ARE QUICK to judge. Any mistake or indiscretion committed by the Church is met with indignation and protest. After years of patience and reflection we are coming to realize that our initial position was too limited. By a long process of conquest we must *recover* all of the authentic Christian concepts that implacable doubt seems to have destroyed. First of all, we will become acquainted with a *new way of loving*—and of feeling and understanding all things—taught by Christ and the Church.

It surprises those who discover it. An unbeliever reads the Gospel:

> I read, and suddenly—revelation! I read and reread, not understanding everything, but I do grasp one thing: it answers my deepest need. All that I dream of, all that I could dream of is expressed here. Life has a meaning and is moving toward some eternal end. . . . At this moment, I am literally living in Christ.[1]

Another testifies:

> Christ was exactly what I should be, and what I *could* be.[2]

Converts without number give the same testimony: when they awaken to the inspiration of Christ's life, they are electrified. Later we will discuss what this might prove. One thing is certain: the convert does find what he had been groping for.

Human psychology is not simple. There may be an element of illusion in such conversions—suspect complacency, false impressions, hidden weaknesses, a deceptive state of enchantment. The fact remains, however, that the soul's needs have been given a direction for research—the humble attitude of Christ, his dynamic process of fulfillment, the noble freedom of spirit that dispels fear from any experience, the resolution to seek justice, universal understanding. The soul thaws, expands, and becomes loving.

The convert is finally making contact with his true self. At last his most adult qualities are reconciled with the childhood intuitions which are now miraculously coming back to him. His newfound modesty, compassion, and a fundamental purity do not inhibit him from fulfilling his functions as a man. Agape, this new love, yearns for a rectitude of life, which means that his actions are prompted by the deepest needs of man's condition and the right relationship to reality—especially to its center—whatever name we choose to give it.

But, as soon as a desire of this sort is born in a man, he becomes aware of a rupture of harmony which had not been apparent before. A richness is missing—the fundamental innocence of being that belongs to the earth and to men, reaching truth through spontaneous unity with the heart and the all of reality. St. Augustine felt exiled "in the regions of dissimilitude." And many of our contemporaries are saying, "I am worth more than my life; a secret element in me aspires to something beyond my everyday occupations."

We are not dealing here with emotional anxieties—these would probably indicate nothing but a lack of balance properly relevant to psychiatry. However, we will try to keep sight of the true intuition that may be implicit in certain disappointments and certain hopes. To speak of fundamental purity or straightforwardness does not necessarily mean we are thinking of anemic or ineffective men, or a spotlessness incompatible with our real condition.

In the Liturgy of the Church, every element has a special meaning. The candle is a particularly eloquent symbol. It is a tall and immaculate pillar made of a chosen material— pure wax, which nourishes the flame. Does this flame seem humble? It is a beginning, the modest presence of a power capable of annihilating all obstacles. The flame which will one day consume the world is kindled. It evokes suns, the whole cosmos, the vital movements of the human heart, the force of thought and action. The fire offered to us comes from the pure white column of wax. On Holy Saturday the celebrant blesses the "new fire," and the deacon sings the marvelous joy of the *Exultet*. It is the benediction of life, restored now to its perfect meaning.

The great and beautiful Paschal candle represents Christ. Its pillar of wax is of a slightly golden white and rises straight and unadorned.[3] Its symbolism could not be more natural. It speaks directly to the soul, evoking a pure grandeur from which the definitive fire springs—the "light to illuminate all nations" that the old man Simeon prophesied. Is it not true that the Liturgy of Holy Saturday, if properly executed, has more impact on the soul than any theatrical drama?

Yet we should not be satisfied with a symbol alone; this would be dangerous. An impression suggests, but does not take the place of, a precise study. As we begin our study, however, let us not forget these impressions. The liturgical ceremony recapitulates the life of Christian peoples over the centuries. The actions, the flesh and blood, of an individual and collective history are expressed here in condensed form. The full range of innumerable actions is rendered in a single sign.

One may doubt the existence of God. One may question

whether he has played a role in human history. Yet even if we embrace one or the other of these ideas, we may still question the transcendence of agape, its truly divine origin, asking ourselves whether the Christian language does not suffer somewhat from an excess of hypothetical concepts. These objections should not blind us to the kernel of truth in the doctrine of agape. We cannot deny the existence of a superior form of love, one which is unearthly and which belongs to the level of riches which we have called "eternal." Here is a fact so important that all controversy over the statutes of this love is secondary. Such controversy is even detrimental if it diverts our attention and thus dissipates our forces. We need all our strength to embrace this mode of loving wherever it can be touched.

But at this point the true form of agape is only partially known. In the course of history religious men have expressed it in marvelous ways; yet they account for only a few of its possible forms of expression, and hardly those needed by our age. St. Paul, St. Francis Assisi, and other religious workers I could cite are not alone in manifesting divine love. It goes beyond that. Agape is *dispersed:* unbelievers can harbor real elements of it—in their sense of truth or justice, for example—and the whole of agape is never present in any one man or group. It is also dispersed in time, for certain of its old forms cannot be exactly reproduced and many new forms have yet to be invented.[4]

Perhaps the first condition for spiritual life is a preparation of oneself for a recasting of one's being, as drastic a recasting as is necessary. But is this not also a prerequisite for the project of verifying the soundness of one's faith? The person who fears the religious experience and wants to reduce it to a minimum seems to manifest a characteristic weakening. We might call it a falling into a middle-class mentality—bearing in mind that this mentality is not confined to any one social category—or to a state of becoming fixed. This dilemma is expressed by Father Surin:

> Let us go, love, into the fiercest storm
> That the Ocean can bring upon me.
> I would much prefer to lose myself with courage
> As I follow you, than to save myself without you.

. . . . .

> I would much rather be unjustly blamed
> By cautious men who fear to perish
> Than to risk nothing, conquer nothing,
> As I take great pains to preserve my soul.[5]

Setting out in search of agape often means that the old man within us will warn that we are about to lose everything. But if we are to reach a new stage of life, we must leave the old behind. Our desires must be inclined toward another order and a crossing over, toward the long and necessary apprenticeship. We must not fear breaking with our habits, but at the same time we must be wary of all doubtful spiritual orientation. For many noble experiences are strengthened by failures; we do not have to destroy our personalities and the laws governing the development of man's nature. Progress, if it is to be real, must merge with our real state of being, leaving our true aspirations and our potentialities intact. We do not strike out willy-nilly in any direction—we should let the evidence accumulate and then follow the lines it seems to indicate. But its voice will be soft and barely audible; he who does not know how to listen will accomplish nothing.

Christ provides and requires such a sharp change of plan for every human life that adherence to the new order is impossible without some degree of magnanimity. He is sometimes rather abrupt in pointing this out to those who wish to pattern themselves on the new order.[6] The greatest saints sometimes had the impression that they had cast themselves into the void, and this they had to accept with faith. All purely human love and the old ideas must be abandoned, without really knowing what lies ahead. But a summons has been given us, and it is one we should heed.

The ordinary result of spiritual impasse is boredom, one of the feelings most foreign to the Gospel. But an impasse will express itself in different ways. A human life may be conducted in serenity and calm and still be in no danger of falling into confined spiritual attitudes. On the other hand, the passionate turbulence which shocks conservative souls is sometimes the very thing which brings on the growth of agape. Then again, certain people may seem to lead highly eventful lives and yet be disturbed at heart.

The lamentable relapse of Christians is quite often due to their knowing neither how to involve themselves with the world nor how to liberate themselves from its bondage. We must attain both involvement and liberation. And even those who feel that they cannot subscribe to all the affirmations of the Church can, through a rigorous undertaking, accept the way of love inspired by Christ. This is an extremely important thought to bear in mind.

I consider, therefore, that Christianity has a kernel of excellence which, once we have glimpsed it, lies beyond the scope of our particular line of questioning. In itself it is sure and solid; and however indefinable it may seem to us to be, once we have made every effort to grasp it, a purified and stabilized discussion will be possible. Yet it is obvious that we cannot resolve everything by this. Early Christianity displayed admirable virtues and a sort of collective spiritual power which was both explosive and gentle. But it allowed many fantasies to creep into its clearest perceptions; and this sometimes altered the content of the truths of the early Church: belief in the imminent Parousia,

naïve representations of the reign of Christ,[7] the attribution
of diseases to demonic possession, etc.

Thus the problem of religious *knowledge*—that is, of
speculative truth—has not been settled. This glance at initial
certainties does not justify a statement of critical value. To
make such a statement, we would have to go back over the
facts in a methodical manner and decide what conclusions
could be drawn—and this must be reserved for another
work. What we have seen so far, however, does enable us
to carry on the discussion at its proper level. A boundary
has been established, pinpointing the real problem. And,
more important, we no longer face the spiritual order
empty-handed; we begin to know what to look for, and
we already possess a degree of spirituality. If we can lead
a profoundly religious life, albeit with uncertainty, we will
not have to force the quest—and perhaps we will attain a
true freedom of mind.

The noetic basis can be sought in two directions:

1. We can conduct the examination on the basis of the
knowledge contained in the religious *experience*. This is
essentially the experiencing of a spiritual *effectiveness,* that
is, of a truth of life yet to be defined and criticized.

What will this method yield? Both much and little—a few
conclusions still rather general in nature but of major
importance. A subtle, passionate, and limited quest.

2. Sooner or later we will be led to reflect on the *history*

of early Christianity. Jesus did speak (and to a certain degree we can rediscover what he said); certain events did take place.

Will we find the essential here? Actually it is impossible to go very far into a historical study without making broad assumptions: these are often unconscious or confused, and always rigid. Purely exegetic discussions usually lead to an impasse, unless the parties involved are in agreement from the beginning. Exegetes will cite identical texts to support differing conclusions. Why? The answer is simple: without realizing it, they have already taken sides on the problem of Revelation, the problem which decides everything.

Therefore, we must conduct an unhurried search for legitimate assumptions, for accurate assumptions which preserve the fine points of the certainties we already possess. A careful reading of religious experiences should allow us to begin with a solid foundation. But we are not ready yet to deal with such problems. One is tempted to go too quickly, to neglect the preliminaries, to build the walls before the foundation.

First—and this is not simple—we must choose the method as a whole made up of constituent parts. We must determine the spirit of the operation and the seeker's attitude toward the religious problem. This will determine the spirit of the operation and the seeker's attitude toward the religious problem. This will indicate the technical means for conducting the investigation. How can we choose a point of departure which will not prejudice our findings? Where will we find a rather hardheaded intelligence prepared to seize the truths in any difficult hypothesis?

NOTES

1. Quoted by R. Girault, *Pour un catholicisme évangélique* (Editions Ouvrières, Paris, 1959), p. 16.

2. *Ibid.,* p. 31.

3. The Paschal candle loses its suggestive meaning if embellished with ornaments and gilt—it should remain completely unadorned.

4. However, we must seek the tone proper to those forms of agape which have been achieved. It is expressed in a remarkable manner in Chapters 5, 6, and 7 of the Gospel according to St. Matthew, in the discourse after the Last Supper, in the account of the Passion according to St. John, and in Chapter 13 of St. Paul's Epistle to the Romans. Perhaps the most outstanding elements are strength and tenderness combined, freedom of soul, and profound solidity. On reading these texts, we must obviously look to the great saints of all the ages for the truest understanding of agape, provided we are able to grasp the personalities of these men and provided they are not misrepresented by biographers. We must distinguish the authentic movement of the soul from its hypocritical imitations and conventional feelings; St. Paul was already aware that a pseudo-charity was possible (Romans 12, 9; II Corinthians 6, 6), and even the great saints at their purest had elements of mental inflexibility and inadequacy.

5. The whole poem is quoted in Book No. 6 of *Dieu vivant* (Editions du Seuil).

6. As in Luke 9, 57–62; Matthew 8, 19–22.

7. A very curious tradition is reported by St. Irenaeus who claims to have had it from the Apostle John through the sole intermediary of Papias. *Adversus Haereses,* V, XXXIII, 3–4. See Fliche and Martin, *Histoire de l'Eglise,* p. 6, n. 1.

II
The Choice of a Method

4. CHOOSING
A POINT OF DEPARTURE

THE PROCESS OF verifying the soundness of one's faith must not, and cannot, be rushed. Our aim at this point is to make a good start. We can hope that once sound premises have been established, the process will be pursued as a collective effort. This will happen when a sufficient part of humanity has recognized the proper method. We must first agree on a position from which to launch the process, agree on what we accept as established knowledge, on what we mean by verifying the soundness of faith, on what the mind strives for and what it rejects.

Certain attitudes which I consider inacceptable have nonetheless persuaded good minds. Such attitudes exaggerate a true idea and focus on only one facet of the problem. In examining a clear but oversimplified concept, other requirements of the question will come to light, requirements which can only be satisfied by other concepts.

How can I expect to understand Christianity if I do not partake of its spiritual riches, if I do not enter into the special movement of the soul which belongs to our faith? Can we talk to a blind man about color? If we are to understand a text in the Gospel, we must know what the words meant in Palestine at the time they were spoken, but we must also be able to appreciate their special resonance when they came from Jesus' mouth.

Therefore, some degree of adherence to the inner movement of Christianity goes to make up the foundation and the sound method, for it clarifies the meaning of the texts and the weight of the religious act. But just what sort of adherence is necessary? Must we declare our belief in the truth of the dogmas? If so, we fear that the question will be prematurely resolved even before it has been formulated.

THE WILL-TO-BELIEVE: BASIC FORM

A position taken by many, though not all, Catholics accentuates this difficulty. It places the will to believe at the base of all religious reflection: belief in the Church as it demands to be believed in; consequently, belief in the veracity of the defined dogmas—the canons of the Ecumenical Councils and *ex cathedra* definitions of the Popes. The reasoning is this: religion is good; we would be lost without it; to enter into it, to receive all of it, we must commit ourselves wholeheartedly to the conditions laid down by the Church. But is this a framework in which we can try to demonstrate the soundness of faith? Yes, reply the upholders of the theory. We think this deserves some reflection.

The theory of the will-to-believe stresses the role of the will in all intellectual choice. Man elects to ask himself certain questions, to interest himself only in certain aspects of a given problem; he commits himself to one side, neglecting another side. He exercises freedom. Intellectual reflection is only one of the elements involved, and is the manifestation of free choice. Such choice is inevitable, even if it is not conscious, for all reflection has as its foundation a whole construct of previous ideas, and a project, an aim, an end. If this is so, then the choice to believe, we are told, has the same value as any other choice. Furthermore, it is justified by its beneficial results: it then appears to be particularly reasonable. Even in intellectual matters it provides illumination, an explaining principle, unparalleled certainty, unity. Human life and all things take on an intensity of meaning that they do not otherwise have.

Several points merit discussion. There seems to be some ambiguity as to the role of freedom and will in intellectual reflection. Let us draw a distinction between the freedom to formulate a problem and the freedom to predefine its solution—between the decision to accept any conclusion that turns out to be true and the decision to admit only that which conforms to a position one has adopted. Freedom of action does not replace objective evidence, but it should serve the latter. Probably in religious matters there can be no evidence without a free act of acceptance; the person who rejects *a priori* does not see. But eventual acceptance is not affirmation. It takes a free act to perceive; any other sort would mean a blind decision, a disregarding of one's own ignorance. There is a freedom which, in its attempt to examine the soundness of a given matter, remains open to eventual revisions, including, if necessary, a reshuffling of basic concepts. And there is a freedom that takes a definite stand at the very first. The necessity for free action at the beginning does not mean that this second form is preferable.

All reflection implies assumptions which may have great scope and flexibility, but which should not be postulated as the solution to a problem. How can we distinguish between two basic affirmations—such as the spiritual fertility of the Church and its dogmatic infallibility? Are they both equally justified?

The authenticity of a position from which to verify the faith rests upon the sum of its consequences: perfection of life, intelligibility, and the inner consistency of the concept itself. Without denying such an argument its due as material supporting certain conclusions, we must determine its scope and limits. Does it authenticate the whole of what we believe? It seems that instead of possessing exactitude in every detail, we are assured of a fundamental truth, one which may have been transposed, explained in uncertain terms. Christianity is a unity, just as the earth and sky form a unity —the sap is good, but nothing is verified at the level of the leaves or even the branches unless one goes into a technical study, and that is another argument and another method. Our certainty would be much greater if we carried out the process on *this side* of definite affirmations,[1] and this would not necessarily mean that subsequent checking could be dispensed with.[2]

The first part of our study, while not claiming to exhaust the question, leads us to think that in matters of doctrine clear-cut elements can only establish rather hazy conclusions. It is the process itself, in its structure and method, that will enable us to justify more definite affirmations. Neither the facts known prior to this process nor any established unity are a valid guarantee of the doctrine, save for a fundamental truth, which is still much too general. A hypothesis which is self-consistent can be false. Are we sure that a different dogma would not be still clearer and more intelligible and satisfy the sum of known facts?

In other words, could we *really* satisfy modern man's desire to demonstrate the soundness of faith by the will-to-believe in its unmodified form and by the refusal to question the dogmas further, whatever the future evidence?

We could develop these different points at great length, but it might become rather academic and tedious. No doubt it would be better to sketch out the position that we find preferable, another position (one at least) which is also legitimate.

SUSPENDED ADHERENCE

To verify the soundness of faith, there are two requirements which must be satisfied:

1. To achieve a deep-seated adherence to the best in Christianity in a way that allows us to understand it and to profit from all of its illuminations.

2. To keep the mind perfectly free; to affirm nothing without solid justification; to adapt the affirmation to the certainties sustaining it; to never call something certain that is doubtful.

We must find, then, an attitude of mind that allows us to contact the unverified content of Christianity without actually accepting it.

The two requirements are compatible, and both are in harmony with the spirit of the Gospel. A proper structuring of the original position will lead to the solution. We will not begin without making assumptions, for that is impossible; but we will begin without prejudices and hypotheses, or they will not be definitive. The basic affirmation will focus on the benevolence of Christianity, not on the truth of its dogmas. No doubt the spiritual richness of the Christian movement implies some speculative truth; while we may glimpse it at the beginning—and how elusive it is!—we will not try to define it in advance. The whole problem will be to bring it into sharper focus by dependable methods.

We unconditionally choose to serve true religious values and to present no obstruction to truth, and, of course, to admit to anything proven to be the word of God to the degree and in the sense that there is a divine word. An effort of total sanctification should go hand in hand with intellectual reflection. Practice of charity and humility, contemplation, prayer, are accessible to all—including the doubter.

It is advisable to postpone taking a position on the dogmas; this would hardly mean that we reject them but, rather, that we avoid prejudicing the assertions of the critical mind—in other words, avoid confusing the unverified with the verified. The technical solution is a suspension of judgment, akin to a phenomenological *epoche*. But the mind can achieve this in many different ways. This point may be difficult to understand at first sight, but on reflection it becomes very simple. It is of major importance, for it makes our method acceptable to the believer as well as to the unbeliever.

Let us begin by considering the case of a person who

firmly believes in the truth of the Church's formal definitions. This commitment of his does not hinder him from
embarking on the task of verifying the soundness of his
belief. He desires to effect a "return" or renewal of his
spontaneous faith, promoting it to a more demanding intellectual level. He cannot be asked to give up his faith in
order to test it, to cancel it for the sake of being more
methodical. This would be a Cartesian type of exaggeration,
and no believer could consent to it. He will retain total
adherence to the content whose soundness has not yet been
established (and no dogma's content is, at the outset). But,
at the beginning, his affirmation will not be on a critical
level—that is all. We can hope, however, that he will be
truly ready to admit to any truth, even if it should modify
his initial position.

As for the partial believer, the person who hesitates or
accepts only some parts of the dogma, he has nothing to
change in a quantitative sense; he, too, will distinguish the
unverified from the verified. Only that which can be verified, in degrees or as a whole, will call for his unqualified
endorsement.

Indeed, the mind is flexible enough to operate on different
levels of understanding with respect to a single subject. A
medical student knows his own body, its resources, its weaknesses, its caprices; he has a sensory and immediate knowl-

edge of it, one which may not be scientific but which is probably quite reliable. To learn the detailed functioning of the organs, he does not have to do away with what he already knew. Or again, a group of people are witnesses to a demonstration in the streets; later one of them studies this event with the aid of documents, photos, a film. With only a little effort he can keep his two levels of knowledge separate. In both cases, regardless of whether one trusts the first level of impressions, the second exists independent of it.

There is a great temptation, however, to transpose initial convictions into critical certainties. It is important to recognize this danger and to be on the lookout for it.

The believer will thus use care and discernment in his approach to the verification process, qualities which are not required by the will-to-believe in its basic form. The telling difference is this: the believer is now ready to receive any truth, even if it would lead to a recasting of his initial conviction. In other words, the believer does not have to suspend his judgment on the truth of the dogmas in order to approach the process of establishing the soundness of faith, but he will do well to judge them on a critical level.[3] He will not extend this to include his belief in the process itself, or cast it as a premise which possesses critical faculties and which is therefore capable of countering all objections in

advance. This theory not only affirms the truth of the dogmas through spontaneous faith; it affirms them as the point
of departure in our search for verification—itself allegedly
a critical process. This difference changes the attitude and
range of the undertaking considerably.

Although we have just stressed the rather complex situation of the believer, in this present study we are particularly
concerned with the speaker who "does not know" whether
or not the dogmas are true. This makes things simpler, and
suspension of judgment can be fully achieved. His case
is a common one today. He is not committed to beliefs he
must maintain.[4] He studies the dogmas, tries to gain better
understanding of them, considers them at length, becomes
permanently imbued with their spiritual essence. But he does
not affirm them as either true or false. He makes inquiry
into what is there.

THE FUNDAMENTAL PRINCIPLE

The attitude of suspended adherence which we propose is
the direct application of the principle that St. Thomas expressed in these terms: *Non crederem nisi viderem esse*

credendum—"I would not have believed if I had not *seen* that belief is necessary."[5] In the beginning it is not an act of will but a "view" that is established, that is, a certainty of the intellect.

Man's vital dynamism brings about the act of seeing. But this act has its limitations.[6] There is also an intelligence of the heart, that is, an illumination of reason by love and insight stemming from adherence to the good. The act of knowing is inseparable from a choice, a receiving, a reverence, and possibly an unreserved giving. But how much of the truth do we see when we practice this giving? The will can furnish the conditions that permit the act of seeing, and without this act there could be no establishing the soundness of faith. It would be disastrous to see only what we have already made up our minds to see; but having situated ourselves in the best conditions for knowing the truth, we should believe—if we have seen that we should. Affirmation in matters of truth presupposes a certainty of the intellect.

But, according to St. Thomas, once we have accepted the initial certainty, we are automatically led to believe in the Church. Evidently this is an immediate effect, without extensive reflection (one need not agree with St. Thomas here). Only in the second phase of the process does the will compel the intellect to believe all of the dogma, although the dogmas are not demonstrable or obvious in themselves—

for example, the Real Presence in the Eucharist. If will controls intellect concerning particular dogmas, it is only in applying a general *view*. The intellect's role is still first.[7]

Therefore, I will hold to this extremely important principle of St. Thomas: the original position essentially consists in a certainty of the intellect, not in a choice of the will.

As I doubt that initial certainty has a direct bearing on the truth of the dogmas but rather relates to the spiritual value of Christianity, to the enormous benefit afforded by the Church, a suspension of judgment is inevitable. It will last throughout the time period separating the first phase from the second (first phase: original certainty; second phase: the decision to believe, duly justified). If great difficulties arise at this point, if the connection between the established spiritual value and speculative truth is not clear, if the authority of the Church in doctrinal matters is not obvious, if an immense problem is spreading today into areas where our predecessors found no reason for hesitation, then one continues to suspend one's judgment on the truth of the dogmas until such problems are solved.

Did St. Thomas think of conducting a search for justification? I think so, but it was very cursory.[8] If he had felt the need to pursue it at greater length, he would have undertaken, between his first and second phases, a thorough investigation whose logical law he would have defined (obviously, as regards the dogmas, a law of uncertainty). The Thomistic analysis of the human act does indeed imply this inquiry—it is applicable, we know, to the act of belief, but it is prior to the will-to-believe.

We must choose: either we reject the principle *Non crederem nisi viderem esse credendum,* or we accept a prolonged uncertainty—possibly one of indefinite duration because a knot of difficulties unseen by St. Thomas introduces new complexities to the problem. If we do not want to renounce the project of verification, we must study the problem with patience.

Suspended adherence is nothing other than St. Thomas' position plus a development of the inquiry. Here a remark should be added: the kind of suspended judgment that seems reasonable to me is strictly limited to the dogmatic level. It does not concern a meta-dogmatic truth accessible through the dogmas but independent of their specific content. This higher truth can only be suggested.[9] Here, I hope, the unconvinced reader will at least see a question meriting study.

Part Two: The Choice of a Method

THE WILL-TO-BELIEVE: MODIFIED

Let us consider again the theory of the basic will-to-believe, in the extreme form in which we first presented it. Is it guilty of the fideism which has been condemned by the Church? Any alert theologian will proceed with care: asserting the primacy of will is contestable and contrary to St. Thomas' principle. But we can improve the theory of the will-to-believe without reducing its consequences; thus the debate quickens and becomes very significant in light of the ultimate options it offers the spirit.

A theologian will admit the principle *Non crederem nisi viderem esse credendum,* but he combines the first two phases—initial certainty, decision to believe—into a single concrete act. One makes one's decision at the beginning of the process: one believes. The theologian claims that this choice is not arbitrary, but founded on the sum of the experienced and the known.

The theologian lays stress on a very true idea: when a thinking being grasps an authentic premise, he does not do so through rational means. "Anything that serves as a foundation is obscure," says Jaspers. A certainty which is a *videre,* knowledge, supports us; we may be unable to explain it, unable to define it (it is too rich and obscure), yet able to realize that it justifies the will-to-believe. In this conception the will-to-believe is not absolutely primary, though it is present from the beginning of the inquiry—there is a first phase virtually distinct from the order of the will.

This plan is acceptable in that it avoids the strong objection which could be raised against the first theory—the primacy given to will. But it brings up other objections.[10] A mind conscious of the problems of this age will still be dissatisfied, for such a modified concept of the will-to-believe does not deal with the principal question: Do the really secure religious certainties guarantee the infallibility of the Church's doctrines or guarantee, indirectly, the literal truth of dogma?

Our basic objection to the proposed concept is that it *denies beforehand, and without sufficient investigation, even the possibility that such complex difficulties exist,* difficulties which many people are aware of today. There are probably many problems which lie between fundamental religious certainty and the decision to believe. Will we purposely choose to ignore them?

Do we, for example, imagine that we could make an unconditional, definitive decision to believe through reason, without studying the documents about Christ, the history of the Christian movement, and eventually the history of other religions too? A spiritual experiencing of Christianity's marvelous effects no doubt justifies spontaneous faith, but a consideration of exegesis and history is necessary to reach a will-to-believe of critical value.

Now the will-to-believe presented to us here is claimed to be absolutely definitive and irrevocable. It is the first step in the process by which we demonstrate the soundness of faith, and it is thought to be superior to the process itself. But would we be pursuing the process properly if we did not take the trouble to examine just how far this firsthand experience goes in establishing firm conclusions, experience which, we are told, justifies us in our decision to believe?

To put it in more concrete terms, by choosing to believe the dogmas, we are taking a position on speculative truth. Specifically, we are taking a position on spiritual matters, committing ourselves to a certain path, partaking of the Church's spiritual resources; but we are also making an intellectual affirmation with regard to truth. Are we sure that experienced and known facts contain a degree of certainty sufficient to justify such a conclusion—to guarantee the infallibility of the Church? And can we be sure without a painstaking investigation of the initial certainty?

We fear an imbalance in the speculative domain. Our question is legitimate. If we fail to analyze or pinpoint the basic certainties, how can we determine the degree of adherence they justify? Either we must renounce the project of verification, or we must recognize that this is one of the areas, perhaps the main one, where verification should be carefully exercised.

If we can critically affirm the truth of the dogmas before beginning the process, then the process is of little purpose. If it is not to be a sham, we must admit that the firsthand experience we possess does not justify our taking a definitive and categorical position.

I realize that an objection might be raised here: can't one maintain a *definitive* certainty on two levels? A total, non-technical view has already convinced the believer of the truth of the dogmas or the soundness of Church dogma; afterward his increased understanding will utilize all the resources of modern rationality. According to this view, the believer wants to promote his faith to the level of highly evolved thought with critical faculties; but before initiating this process, faith, such as it is, is already certain.

A doubter will reply that if there is a nontechnical certainty covering the whole doctrinal problem, why search further? That in itself will do. Academic refinements count for little; the question is whether the dogmas are true.[11] Of course, there is a pretechnical certainty, but does it go far enough to guarantee the truth of the dogmas? If the believer is sure, all the better for him.

We only regret that such a man cannot state the foundations of his certainty more clearly. If he were somehow able to do this, be it through so-called rational processes or any other process, we would say he had verified or justified the soundness of his faith. That is all we can ask. Until then we must suspend judgment.[12]

I think, then, that the theory of the will-to-believe, even when qualified as above, cannot be *imposed* on anyone. It is a matter of conscience. There are several legitimate points of departure besides this one.

With these remarks, we again see that a suspension of judgment is really an absence of knowledge in people who doubt. When the believer practices this suspension in the course of the process, is he only making a pretense, one intended to attract the unbeliever and ultimately dupe him? It is better to take a very honest position: certainly, the believer believes and does not have to hide it; but either his verifying process is rigged up by his earlier convictions, or it is undistorted, even if innerly illuminated by them.

The danger to the believer is that he might automatically rediscover his faith in terms of a fictitious verification— many authors down through the ages have naïvely read the ideas of their age into the Gospel. On the other hand, it is possible to develop a process of verification strictly consistent with the premises we have adopted. A dialogue with the unbeliever may help the Christian to purify his process of the intellectual and critical considerations which could intrude upon and falsify the development of a justification. Then the suspension of judgment of even the firmest believer will no longer be an apologetic fiction; it will be an instrument for rigorous thinking, a principle of method to be strictly observed.

RECAPITULATION AND SUMMARY

In summing up, we find that there are several possible points of departure. The whole process of demonstrating the soundness of faith will be influenced by a choice made at the beginning. The entire intellectual life of a person committed to religious questions may hinge on a premise that is not spelled out, one which is merely implicit. For my part, I am convinced of the following:

1. The necessity of participating in the Christian spiritual essence, and in the deepest possible sense, at the risk of failing to understand.

2. The legitimacy of a suspension of judgment on the truth of the dogmas.[13]

No one is silly enough to ask Catholics to stop believing in the dogmas. But the man of today will ask the theologian who claims to be attempting the project of verification: Are you ready to adopt any unforeseen truth? Are you sure that you have not surreptitiously adopted a method that rejects certain eventual truths? Because Christians, as well as the noncommitted, seek real verification—nonfictitious and in a pure form. We must not adopt a method that definitively and irrevocably draws conclusions before any inquiry is made.

The different points of departure can be stated as follows:

I. "Independent" thought, that is, reflection without adherence of any sort to the Gospel and the Church.

This also includes hidden adherence, for there are substitutes for explicit adherence. Could it be said that Gandhi did not enter into Christianity? The very serious danger here is that one may lose the illumination derived from extensive religious experience and the spiritual penetration of the Christian movement.

But if we practice a flexible adherence to Christianity in order to correct this loss, it would be better if it were explicit. Apart from the desirability of setting a straight course for deep values, real familiarity with doctrine is indispensable.

II. Processes starting from an adherence to Christianity.

A. Theories of prior will-to-believe (prior to any extensive research).

1. The will-to-believe in its basic form. A very debatable position, especially because of the primacy given to will.

2. The will-to-believe in partially modified form. The

will is generally subordinated to a certainty; but, the latter not being explicit, it is difficult to know if it really justifies the decision that we make by it. We do not verify the unity of the whole at the beginning, but at the end. The ability of this process to establish reliable conclusions is limited.

3. The will-to-believe in more modified form, an attitude of contingence upon a certainty that we do not refuse to spell out. This position differs from the preceding one, that of St. Thomas, in its thematization of the initial certainty and its explicit study. The only drawback with this concept is its brevity of inquiry. If we accept that the inquiry must be long and difficult, we are led to the following position.

B. Suspended adherence.

Participation in the Christian essence, the source of life and light, is not sacrificed in any way. The process by which the soundness of faith is established, taken in its earnestness and its need for time, is not sacrificed in any way. We need a very special type of adherence, one adapted to a suspension of this kind; research conducted with integrity requires that nothing is asserted as definitive until it has been verified.

NOTES

1. For example, we will believe in the divinity of Christ not because we have committed ourselves to the Church, but only if we can support this belief with facts and reasonably conclusive texts—or if we have sufficient reasons for accepting the Church's word, for believing that its extraordinary magisterium is infallible. It is not necessary to prove each dogma if we can rely on the Church in an overall way. Again, this act must not only be chosen, but founded, at the level of truth—on certainties.

2. A similar question is dealt with in my earlier work, *Le problème de Dieu inscrit dans l'évolution* (Editions du Cerf, Paris, 1963), Ch. VIII: "Limites de l'argument d'intelligibilité."

3. There can be no suspension of judgment except within and at the level of verifying thought. The latter does not use the body of dogma as an affirmed and certain premise; the certainties it depends upon are far more undetermined (cf. Part One and Chapter 5 of this study). The believer does not suspend judgment in the realm of spontaneous precritical conviction.

4. Just what can we adhere to with suspended adherence? To spiritual values; in a general way, to everything we can admit to in Christianity without affirming anything beyond the certainties we possess.

The person who doubts can adhere (1) to the evangelic ideal (even if he still has some reservations or hesitations about the details), taken at its principal axis, yet taken in its whole breadth and intensity; (2) to the real virtues possessed by Christians, to the spiritual values transmitted by the Church; (3) to the content of the elementary religious perceptions, to the initial certainties (cf. Part One and Chapter 5 of this study).

I think that one could also adhere to the *spiritual meaning* of the dogmas without making up one's mind as to their speculative content.

Choosing a Point of Departure

Just as in phenomenology one can retain all that is concrete without holding an ontological position, in a similar way the religious man can retain the whole evangelic ideal and its spiritual inspiration (and the spiritual key which the dogmas provide), without either affirming or denying the speculative element of the doctrine.

5. II. II. 1, 4 *ad* 2 *um: (qui credit) non crederet nisi videret ea esse credenda.*

6. Neither St. Thomas' thought nor ours establishes a definite distinction between the actions of the intellect and those of the will. Indeed, these actions are interdependent. The operation of the intellect is effective in the human being's movement toward his end. Desire for the ultimate end is the motivating force of the whole process. But the desire to know truth must assist us in our desire for the ultimate end. The operation of the intellect demands a strict guarantee of objectivity as well as the supremacy of reason in its own domain.

7. For St. Thomas, as we know, will is a sort of love, an appetite of the intellect. Thus the exercise of will presupposes an awakening: a known reality is desired as good. One must first "see" that the act of belief is good, and it is only good if the Church really does express the word of God. We must, therefore, see and verify that God speaks through the Church.

(The will can only precede and activate the intellect if the will is directed toward the supreme end or toward good in general, with the intellect, as a particular power, having a determined act [I. 82, 4, *ad* 1 *um*].)

8. A page at the beginning of *Contra Gentiles* (I, VI).

Note this formula: "Fidelity imparts faith to a man, not insofar as he is man, but insofar as God makes use of him to spread his word. This is easy to verify with reliable indications" (III, *Sent. d.* 23, *q.* 2, *a.* 2, § 2, *ad* 3 *um*). St. Thomas evidently felt little need to make these simple and reliable points explicit; we see here the wide gulf between the modern mind and that of the Thirteenth Century.

9. Cf. Part One and Chapter 5 of this study. A special study of the dif-

ferent dogmas would bring it out in more definite terms.

10. See earlier discussion in this Chapter.

11. Or if the act of belief is justified, which comes to the same thing.

12. This seems to agree with St. Thomas' position: he does not maintain that belief is necessary *before inquiry*. This conclusion stems from the inquiry (whether it is brief or long does not alter the problem's form).

13. In my opinion, this suspension will be limited to the obvious or literal definition of the dogma—since meta-dogmatic truth is beyond all question.

5. TAKING HOLD AT LAST?

I WOULD LIKE NOW to discuss an experience which is on the whole familiar to all Catholics. At times it is unexpectedly intense, and hence particularly illuminating. It might contribute something new to the questions we have been considering. We must be ready to reexamine everything when the need arises, and to do so without panic.

In moments of lucidity we sense the *spiritual wealth* of the Christian movement and of Christianity's principal organ, the Catholic Church. We often take stock of the Church's faults at the same time. There are many. But this hardly matters anymore. We are concerned with something else, and this "something" has an indescribable value.[1] This experience, whatever feelings accompany it, entails an intellectual perception—a forceful integration of the facts in our possession.

We cannot really define or assess this truth, but we can try to move toward its center. In general, a person who reaches a deeper understanding of Christianity is sure to

find a foundation of extraordinary stability in frank adherence to the Church, a foundation that gives life meaning and makes for accurate thinking in religious questions.
First we perceive the naïve, superficial, and impure elements
in all other pathways. Then we appreciate the value of the
path laid down by the Church, despite its many blunders.
It is the height at which the true grandeur of Christianity
is located that is so striking. Usually we seek it on too low a
level; and likewise, if we quarrel with the Church, we usually do so on a plane where it is indeed vulnerable.

First of all, one grasps the contribution of Christ himself
rather than that of his disciples: it is *Christ* who answers
man's principal problem. We sense the tone set by the
Gospel—the quality of the pathways we uncover. The
Gospel—which is the fact of Christ—constitutes the source,
and the rest is subordinate to it. But without the Church,
where on earth today would we find the spiritual impulse
born of Jesus? The Christian movement forms an indivisible
whole. Whatever the possible points of argument (and they
are endless), the Church nonetheless continues to perpetuate
the influence of Christ.

Moreover, once we perceive the wealth of sanctity and intelligence within Christianity, strong adherence becomes a
necessity. Not only to reach the shores of peace and stability,
but to possess the vital truth. We are standing in darkness, a

rather ineffable truth in our hands. Our conception of it is probably naïve; possibly we confuse it with what surrounds it, but it is nevertheless better to be dealing with a diamond, even though it may be encased in an imperfect matrix. The danger is to let the essential slip through our fingers, to err dreadfully.

To see this is rather like being struck by lightning! It is the fire and the rock; it is gentleness and unfailing strength. Hidden fire, solidity, power, invisible warmth—felt in calm and in silence as an unsurpassable reality.

At such moments we understand a fact of great import-ance to problems of faith, namely, that *the essential is not taking place at the level of reasons formulated by man.* For our intellects are not used to functioning at the necessary height. These realities can only be reached by a great leap. This leap, based on an unreserved adherence to the Church, can place us there. We wonder if it is possible to rise to it any other way.

The long-sought justification of the act of faith should be placed at this height, there where we encounter meaning and where human life and intellect are wonderfully strength-ened. But at this level almost nothing can be said. This is one of the reasons why the apologetic attempts to date seem insufficient. What we manage to say has little connec-tion with the only justification equal to the task.

Does what we encounter at this level offer, to an authentically critical mind, confirmation of the whole of Christian belief? It seems quite certain that the answer is "no." Our experience with the higher reality clears the ground and situates the problem; it does away with many petty difficulties and false questions. But it does not resolve everything. Let us look at this more closely. Without claiming to define the ineffable, we can sketch its main outline:

1. We measure the benefit—a rather personal and private one—which adherence to Christ and the Church imparts to a human being.

2. We measure the power and stability of the Church as a spiritual institution; we gauge the immensity of this torrent of life and the dangers of isolating ourselves from it.

3. We understand the spiritual conditions for wholesome reflection on religious questions. Just as the method is at least half of the philosophy, there are only a certain number of roads which will bring one to the truth of spiritual doctrines. Careful consideration of the dogmas is a must; one should be in the habit of using them to grasp the superior reality we have glimpsed. We understand the *intellectual* dangers of dissociating ourselves from the doctrinal views of the Church—these are penetrated by the superior reality in question, and express it eloquently. Clearly, however, this does not yet prove the speculative truth of the dogmas.

4. The specific benefits one derives from Christianity, the true character of our experience, the nature of the superior reality we have glimpsed, are bound up with our recognition that the Real enjoys a certain level of unity.

Let us explain ourselves on this important point. According to traditional Christian thought, the Real contains an astonishing degree of richness and harmony. There is a God who thinks and loves; there is the Revelation, the Incarnation, the Eucharist, and so forth.

Reality is unpredictable and wonderful; yet for many of our contemporaries it is hardly more than a game of chance, a physiochemical function, a successive exchange of energy, a structure without aim soon to be destroyed. Here are two points of view. Everything—life and thought—is transformed according to the initial conviction we adopt. Our choice really determines our findings, particularly when we argue about the dogmas or exegetic questions; initially we either believe or do not believe in a degree of meaning and unity which makes the dogmas possible.

If humanity is governed by God's design, and if this design is as closely woven into the fabric of the world as Christians think it is—no doubt the design must correspond to the type that Christians conceive—then it is very easy to admit Christ's virginal birth and his divine presence in the Eucharist. But this would be impossible if one considered the world absurd. One of the historical tasks of the Church has been to maintain, through its dogmatic assertiveness, the idea of reality's *grandeur*.

Is this only a hypothesis? Does the above experience merely illustrate the benefits derived from believing in it? In this connection it seems to me that we can draw the following conclusions: if there is this degree of meaning in the Real, it is quite hidden; in order to perceive it, we must surmount nonsense and absurdity. Thus a degree of meaning and knowledge is plausible, because it is harmonious with the sum of religious and human experience—provided the life of man is itself raised to a certain level of unity and meaning.

The quality of life legitimatizes a belief in the quality of the Real, and vice versa. It seems almost impossible to lead a strong and meaningful life without a sharp sense of a real foundation which initiates and sustains a heroic—or, in the full sense of the word, charitable—existence. Could rewards of this kind be compatible with complete illusion? With some illusion, certainly (absolute conviction does miracles); but with total illusion, it is hardly possible: not only does the idea of a concealed fullness of the Real agree with what is experienced and known, but it has the eminent value of explanation.

St. Augustine said, "The Christian mysteries, though obscure in themselves, are the source of clarity."[2] History becomes comprehensible, from its least vicissitudes to its totality, when we perceive the development of the world as man's relationship with God. Individuals and groups progressively define themselves in relation to God, choosing, consciously or unconsciously, their connection with the Absolute in concrete terms. A more comprehensive intelligibility of all things is discovered thereby. There was an unexplained essence at the heart of things; now it has become clear. The final word is spoken, or allows itself to be glimpsed. A new dimension, a new area of intelligibility, is attained.[3]

I am led to conclude, therefore, that there is a true perception in this experience—we see the concrete possibility that a human life might maintain a previously unhoped-for degree of consistency, and we also begin to see a real foundation for this possibility.

This experience does not yet guarantee, however, that the system of dogmas expresses the unity of the Real in its own terms. Let us admit that we have seen it at the level where it exists; the dogmas have at least the merit of suggesting a consistent reality, consistent to just the necessary degree—and this through a point we may not have thought of: the relation to God, connection with the divine. This is all that we can say.[4]

The experience, therefore, definitely has its speculative side and constitutes a (rather indirect) trial concerning the structure of the Real and its ultimate nonabsurdity. It does not enable us to specify the method and the technical means by which the degree of perceived meaning comes into being. The truth of the dogmas becomes plausible, yet is not confirmed by the experience itself. We are dealing with a foundation of truth rather than an exhaustive study of properties.

All in all, the experience confirms us in our first position: if we are not to renounce the project of verification, an inquiry is necessary. Before undertaking it, we must cultivate an attitude which combines deepened adherence with a suspension of judgment on a level which is secondary but which nonetheless pertains to dogma.

The remarks in this chapter bring to a close our definition of the term "suspended adherence": it is *the complete acceptance of the epistemological situation* corresponding to the experience described. It is intense and serene fervor, total will to truth, assessment of the known and the unknown. We expect a full perception of Christianity, the decision to adhere to everything really spiritual, and the refusal to cheat with the remaining problems.

Taking Hold at Last?

NOTES

1. This calls to mind Pascal's famous message: Certainty, Joy, Peace, etc.
2. *Credo ut intelligas.*
3. This question is treated in somewhat the same manner in my work entitled *Le problème de Dieu inscrit dans l'évolution,* where the hypothesis of a Source of meaning gives an additional intelligibility to phenomena. And, once again, we are led to the same central question: How much can one conclude from such an argument? (Cf. *ibid.,* Ch. VIII.) I believe the conclusions one can draw are both real and limited.
4. We might ask, however, whether this approach does not imply the existence of a *conscious* God. Without it one could envision a vaguer deity (and many philosophers have done so). But a high degree of meaning, which seems to be best interpreted as a personal relationship to God, presupposes that the Absolute is endowed with thought and will. In a delicate matter such as this one, where proof is impossible, this approach should be given serious consideration.

6. FAITH

Does the concept of suspended adherence pass over one of Christianity's essential principles, the necessity of faith? This is a vital question, and brings us to some important clarifications.

A critic might simply say, "Your project is contradictory. You want to adhere, but adherence is achieved through faith. You must choose: either no adherence, or no suspension of judgment."

Actually, we have already answered this objection: one must have a basis or foundation for the initial act; one must also have some real certainty about the evidence which forms the basis of the act. Our task is to adjust our adherence to the epistemological situation we face. How limiting if one said, "Adherence with full belief or no adherence at all!" The ideal is to have just the right degree of adherence.

But Christians have always thought that the indispensable illumination leading to true religious knowledge is bound up with faith—the entrance key to the kingdom of Christ.

We seek to enter, that we might gain understanding. And what does this require? Faith. Now if the word did not have different meanings, the question would be insoluble. We will solve the dilemma simply by referring to the Bible. This will help us to clear up the point of ambiguity that complicates the problem.

BIBLICAL CONCEPTION OF FAITH

We cannot help but be struck by the breadth of the concept *faith* as presented in the Gospel. It goes far beyond our usual understanding of the term—a belief, the intellect's adherence to a doctrine.[1] It is very important that we rediscover its meaning and the mental structure behind this.

The idea of faith comes down to us from the Old Testament, drawing together intuitions of wonderful richness. These must be considered first, however briefly.

Left to himself, man is a miserable creature, beset with illusion. He imagines that he is capable of attaining true happiness, perfection, wisdom. This is his cardinal error. Jahve alone is, in and of himself, good, great, generous, holy, and perfect. These qualities are summed up in the idea of *righteousness,* virtue of the King and of God. Righteousness is also what every good man desires; it is, or will be, the world's new state, due to Jahve. In the thought of the Hebrew people, it was increasingly associated with the notion of saintliness—with an idea of compassion and benevolence, with some kind of joy, and even at times with triumph. But there is only one true righteousness, the one received from Jahve in the image of divine righteousness—any other is mere illusion. There is nothing solid in human life unless it is linked to and receives validity from divine perfection.

"Their righteousness is of me," declares Jahve (Isaiah 54, 17).

". . . the righteousness which is of God by faith" (Philippians 3, 9).

Jahve is the rock of excellence, the greatness that does not fail. All water not drawn from this source will ultimately prove illusory and bitter. We stand in the benevolence of Jahve who offers his gifts with abundance, and here we must find the human attitude capable of fully receiving.

The root *'mn,* which in Hebrew gives us the words faith and belief, has as a primitive meaning "to carry a suckling child." This implies a benevolent care on the part of the supporter and a confident dependence on the part of him who is supported.[2] The substantives *'emounah* and *'emet* (which correspond to the Greek *pistis*) have fairly broad meanings, the central idea being consistency, stable solidity.[3] Faith consists in relying upon the strength of an Other, because this

Other is solid; it means being faithful to him in that he is true—that is, is nonbetraying, nondeceiving. This can be seen in the Second Book of Chronicles: "Believe in the Lord your God, so shall ye be established" (20, 20); or, in more literal terms, "rest on the strength of Jahve and you will be fortified."[4]

Again and again the Bible points out that our souls should strive for loyalty, sincerity, and firm belief in divine protection, even when protection is not apparent. It urges us to be humble.[5] The arrogant mentioned frequently in the Old Testament think that on their own initiative they can find a righteousness that does not come from Jahve; they are not prepared to receive the divine gift.

If all true perfection is bestowed on the world by God, the human being must avoid closing himself to the radiance from above. The flower affirms the sun, blossoming as it opens; thus the religious man worships, and receives life through faith. The highly controversial phrase "the righteous man lives by his faith" is almost a tautology if we remember that righteousness is received from God and that faith, for the human soul, is an act of opening. It is also continuity, steadfastness in union with God, and unwavering fidelity.

Faith seeks the happiness (often an austere happiness) that comes from God, and prefers him to any other (necessarily illusory) source of strength and joy; it does not waver

when the divine Absolute counters our judgments or prefer-
ences. One of the most characteristic actions of faith is adherence to a paradox where God is the guaranty. It means
counting on something unseen, but assured by God, and suffering when God so desires. In the Epistle to the Hebrews
there are compelling examples which illustrate this point.[6]
Today these testimonies may seem to exaggerate the concept
of faith, but they echo similar teachings in the Book of
Psalms, the Book of Prophets, and in Job. And Christ con-
ceives of faith in the same way. The necessity of receiving is
one of the central themes of the Gospel:

> He that receiveth you receiveth me, and he that re-
> ceiveth me receiveth him that sent me. (Matthew 10, 40;
> cf. John 13, 20)

> But as many as received him, to them gave he power to
> become the sons of God. (John 1, 12)

> He that receiveth a prophet in the name of a prophet
> shall receive a prophet's reward; and he that receiveth
> a righteous man in the name of a righteous man shall
> receive a righteous man's reward. (Matthew 10, 41)

The reward is commensurate with the act of receiving,
and the latter with the amount of *flowing in of God* which
takes place in an event or a person. Faith is the readiness to
receive all divine gifts; it is man's ever-faithful response to

all divine initiative with respect to salvation. And the acts expressing faith are extremely varied.[7]

"But if any provide not for his own, and specially for those of his own house, he hath denied the faith, and is worse than an infidel" (I Timothy 5, 8).

Those whom the Gospel praises for their faith are those who are in need and know that they depend upon the good will of God. Herein lies the happiness of the unhappy, exalted by the Sermon on the Mount. The Pharisee believes himself to be righteous—he does not enter into the Kingdom, and keeps others from doing so (Matthew 23, 13). On the other hand, the attitude of faith is comparable to, and perhaps identical with, spiritual infancy; the child does not try to construct his life by his own efforts and to achieve perfection by his own means—he expects everything from those greater than he.

Faith is the act of opening up a human life, conscious of its own needs, in response to God's offer of his gifts. It is the option to turn away from the temptation of vain pursuits and to seek the Absolute; it is preference for saintliness to the point of heroism—and steadfastness in this choice. In short, it is fidelity to God in the greatest sense.[8]

Christian faith returns with renewed ardor to the great initiative of God expressed in the Proclamation concerning Christ and the Apostles. A Word which is life and light descends to the earth; it knows the men of God by the way in which it is received. Some recognize the mark of the divine and venerate it with their whole beings. Others are indifferent—they do not detect the presence of a breath from above, for they do not have a corresponding expectation in their souls; they do not shake off their torpor at the sound of this Word capable of arousing buried religious strivings. Some people raise legitimate but petty objections (the ignorance or naïvete of the Apostles, etc.), and thus remain insensitive to the light. Some denigrate God's manifestation and call the divine satanic; this blasphemy against the Spirit characterizes the soul's closing of itself to the gifts of God.

To have faith means that from now on one will *receive the Word* as the means by which the grace of salvation is transmitted; one will be receptive to the divine virtue which permeates the Christian movement.

Faith is an entrance and the point of departure for a progressive journey which will open up new needs and growth on a more advanced level. Faith is a beginning. St. Paul says that there is an element of expectation inherent in faith, a measure of insufficiency and provisionalism, while charity is a blossoming and a fullness. Faith is always a necessity here on earth because we must continually receive the gift of God and be faithful to him; it is divine agape we receive, which then takes hold and develops. Faith is a stretching outward toward charity, summoning it and making it possible.

This Scriptural concept of faith is so rich and contains such religious truth that the mind is overwhelmed by it. It would be a tragedy to lose this great vision which determines man's condition and defines the first requirement of religion.

FAITH AND BELIEF

The relationship between the act of faith and the act of belief is complex due to the concepts about them in the Old and the New Testament. This subject cannot be dealt with in a cursory manner. *A profound faith is possible even when belief cannot be justified in good conscience.* But it is faith in the Biblical sense (receptivity to the divine gifts, fidelity to God, real regard for Christ's message) that enables one to enter and understand the Christian movement. Since faith is the *principle* of light or spiritual penetration, it is related to a *germinal act* of the spirit, rather than to *conclusions*. That is why suspension of judgment and adherence to Christianity, with all that the latter affords us in the way of clarification, are not contrary attitudes.

If God speaks through the Church, then it is quite clear that we must *believe* the truths spoken by God, even if they surprise us and contradict appearances; our faith would be incomplete if we were to doubt what God asserts. When we believe in elusive truths for the very reason that they have been revealed, we perform an act of theological value; it allies us directly with God, puts us on his side, and allows us to take part in his thought. These points were stressed by medieval theology and seem quite obvious to us today.

We understand that if a word comes from God, it deserves full adherence; a clear affirmation, even if it were fragmentary or disconcerting, would more than satisfy our taste for truth. We would receive a divine word with unspeakable joy and an unparalleled satisfaction in our inmost selves, especially when it related to the most important questions, those bearing on our destiny.

For modern souls the difficulty lies in determining whether or not a word comes from God. And if God has spoken, has he said everything in dogmatic definitions? The innermost content of the divine word may be enveloped in human interpretations. We feel, then, that a very serious question can legitimately be asked of the Church: How do you justify your conviction that God has spoken and that you are the depository of his word? It is natural that certain minds, through an exacting sense of objectivity, do not make a decision about this until they have sufficient reasons for doing so.

A doubter cannot assert that the Church is mistaken. It is not impossible, *a priori,* that God speaks to man. On making a historical analysis, we might decide that the beginnings of Christianity are not sufficiently clear or convincing; but we cannot find any evidence that clearly disproves the idea of a divine Revelation. The history of the Church, its origins and its current life, may contain too many obscure points to allow us to commit ourselves to the idea; but there is certainly no decisive evidence against it. Therefore, if one is searching for truth, it is very important not to exclude the hypothesis that "God has spoken." Besides, a divine word may come to us couched in human ideas.

Classic theology admits that Scriptural inspiration in general respects the normal functioning of the human psyche. God is the guarantor of affirmations that an inspired writer discovers for himself; or, we could maintain, a substratum of divine authority underlies the word of man. An honest and purely scientific mind should be open to any truth, including a revealed truth, if any exists; and no one can be sure that it does not. For those whose vocation is to seek, whose need for absolute truth is a holy obligation, renouncing of verification would be an offense against religion.

It is equally unthinkable that one reject a dogma *a priori*, for example, the divinity of Christ, in that it does not correspond to one's personal opinion. If Christ's divinity is a reality, we should not hesitate to believe in it, or at least to believe in it in the sense in which it is a reality. But we cannot affirm the truth of dogmas through faith in the Biblical sense of the term.[9] It is legitimate to base one's decision on a discussion of historical criticism and to remain uncertain as long as one is not personally convinced.

Doubt is a spiritual exercise, for it presupposes vigilant watch over one's actions and permanent openness to truth. Denial is easy, and the conformist who adopts other people's beliefs for the sake of peace is taking the easy way out. The kind of doubt we are speaking of is a noble exercise of faith. It should leave us completely receptive to the Church, yet allow us, through our sense of the Absolute, to refuse to affirm the soundness of anything we are not sure about.

If this attitude is adopted and faithfully maintained, we are deepened, refined; and the mediocre life which was growing in our souls is changed into gold. Without it (for those who cannot do other than doubt) there would be no faith. It increases one's courage to pursue the truth, doing away with bitterness, disaffection with the Church, and indifference to spiritual matters. If religious certainties are hard to come by, now, having paid for them dearly, we cling to them and are nourished by them, even when they are very incomplete.

Doubt gives us a more direct reference to God—it devalues the intermediaries, not as mediators, but as occasional blocks or impediments. We submit to naked faith, faith stripped of its usual supports, shorn of a mental system that threatens to become another luxury and trap, another bit of property and quasi-temporal structure of thought. We accept the destruction of our thoughts if they are not God's thoughts.

The desire for total purification does not shrink from consequences of any sort, even from inner desolation and the desert of the soul. And if the spirit is torn to pieces, we can still offer God our obedience to his just will; we can still worship him devotedly by means of our inevitable crucifixion, then, even at that moment, calling loudly to him to bring his light. Indeed, there is light and peace, but we do not always know what kind.

NOTES

1. Thus the centurion of Capernaum is humble and has a sense of a world order governed by God, a sense of Jesus as an instrument which brings the divine order into being; this alone prompted Christ to say, "I have not found so great [a] faith, no, not [in any man] in Israel" (Matthew 8, 5–10). The hemorrhaging woman will not give way to despair; she is convinced that salvation is still possible; she believes in the abundance of God's bounty; she calls on his mercy; she also sees Jesus as the instrument of divine benevolence; and thus he tells her, "Thy faith hath made thee whole" (Matthew 9, 20–22). The sinful woman anoints the feet of Jesus; her personal generosity answers God's generosity toward her, especially his act of bringing her into contact with Christ; her faith

consists of a fervent love; her faith saves her (Luke 7, 37–50). The tenth healed leper returns to glorify God; he too is told, "Thy faith hath made thee whole" (Luke 17, 15–19).

2. Cf. Guillet, *Thèmes bibliques* (Aubier, 1951), p. 31, where the roots *hen, 'mn, hesed, 'emet,* are explained.

3. The first meaning of the verb *'aman* is "to bear" (Numbers 11, 12). It evokes the role of the educator and nurse entrusted with the strengthening, support, and shaping of a weak creature (II Kings 10, 1, 5; Isaiah 49, 23; Esther 2, 7, etc.). The *nifal* of the verb means "to support oneself," that is, to stand alone, to be steady, strong, stable. The *hiphil* often means "to believe," and the Septuagint translate it as *pisteuein;* it implies to take support from (to rest one's weight upon) something or someone solid, to depend upon (Isaiah 7, 9; 28, 16: to take support upon the rock; cf. Romans 9, 33 and 10, 11; I Peter 2, 4–6); this has led to the following meanings: (1) *'emet* (solid) or *'amen* (truly, yes) as the response to a reliable and genuine message; (2) to believe, for example, in Genesis 45, 26, Jacob does not believe what he hears concerning his son Joseph; (3) to trust in, to depend upon. While in no way dismissing the intellectual meaning of belief, the verb *'aman* thus derives its religious depth (especially in the Psalms) from a greater idea, loosely: to be nurtured, to depend upon another's strength, to regard as stable. Even the *hiphil* goes beyond the meaning of belief. The substantives and adjectives have a still greater breadth. *'Emounah* means steadfastness, surety, fidelity, trust; *'emet* expresses stability, honesty, integrity, and, in an absolute sense, "a being's essential solidity" (Guillet, *Thèmes bibliques,* p. 41).

4. A play on words, on the *hiphil* and *nifal* of the same verb. Also found in Isaiah 7, 9.

5. "His soul which is lifted up is not upright in him: but the just shall live by his faith" (Habakkuk 2, 4; cf. Romans 1, 13, Galatians 3, 12).

6. Noah is warned of the flood; there are no outward signs that it will take place, yet he believes that it will (Hebrews 11, 7). Moses accepts all divine word without argument "as [if he is] seeing him who is invisible"

(11, 27), and saw God's promise, though still unseen by other men, as true reality. Moses chooses God's plan and God's will; he gives up his claims as the son of the Pharoah's daughter, preferring to suffer with the people of God rather than to receive acclaim estranged from their destiny (11, 25). Through preferring the ways of God, believers have been mocked, have wandered alone, have been tortured, and have perished (11, 35, and following). Jesus, the supreme example of faith, suffered on the Cross because this was the road God set before him (12, 1–4).

7. To open the roof in order to bring the palsied man to Jesus (Mark 2, 5); to anoint the feet of Jesus (Luke 7, 50); to trust in spite of the storm (Matthew 8, 26); to walk on the water without doubting (Matthew 14, 31); to ask for healing (the woman of Canaan in Matthew 15, 28, the blind man in Mark 10, 52); to give glory to God (Luke 17, 19); to believe in Jesus (especially in John 11, 25); to believe the message of John the Baptist (Matthew 21, 32); to believe that Jesus was sent by God (John 11, 42). See I John 4, 16: "and we have known and believed the love that God hath to us."

8. The Biblical concept of faith obviously presupposes the existence of God. But one can take a similar attitude at the very beginning of the verifying process, at the point where one questions God's existence and a definite answer is not given. The most exhaustive questioning need not keep the person who doubts from being receptive to spiritual light: receptivity is an attitude of faith. We will call it "beginning faith."

9. Or in the sense of "beginning faith."

Conclusion

Conclusion

IT IS WELL to deal with the requirements of the mind in a straightforward manner. Christianity will be in danger unless there is a meeting between the thought of the Church and the modern intellect with its sensitive need for truth. We cannot span this gap by intellectual means alone; a considerable amount of pain and fortitude will be required. But neither will we succeed without an intellectual attitude of great purity.

One of the lessons we will learn from the current crisis is that real problems are not solved by temporary measures. Either we leave the problem alone, adjusting to it with modesty (often an excellent solution), or we deal with it in all its implications, first experiencing it, receiving it into ourselves, then allowing a painful maturation to develop until little by little the whole evolves toward light and we find that with the years we—and the problem along with us —are transformed.

Human doubt must be redeemed; the exercise of critical

intelligence is an inevitable function of man, but it can turn into sin. Yet it can be carried on as a holy endeavor, and we must make it just that, without limiting its scope. Priests in particular must deal with this tormenting experience. They are asked to face the trial, but not to sin; to strive to reorient the critical process as it is tempted by chaos.

Indeed, all theologians agree on the need for verification on a critical level, but many impose such restrictions on the point of departure that *real* verification cannot be carried out. This is the crux of the problem. In this study we have considered a common case—doubt concerning probity and religious generosity. People with this sort of doubt do not ask the Church to renounce its dogmas. But they do ask for the right to adjust their adherence to what their conscience can accept. They ask for endorsement of a method of verification that exercises a suspension of judgment (whose scope has been carefully defined).

This brings us to two great, concrete problems; if we cannot solve them completely, at least we have a sound working method for dealing with them.

1. Many people feel that they are rejected by the Church if they do not believe, or if they do not believe everything, even if their doubt is a serious matter, is taken in good faith, and is an absolute necessity to their religious stance. They do not realize that they can share in the Christian body and benefit from its movement. If they could be sure that the

doctrine comes from God, they would accept it joyfully; but they are not sure. They must be shown that adherence is possible and can be maintained without total commitment to beliefs, if this is necessary. For true religion accepts true questioning.

Those who come to the Church in this spirit should be granted entry and given a place. The Church can show them the extreme difficulty of questioning the doctrine, indicate the danger which an unsuspecting mind can fall into in embracing naïve conclusions, and point out the spiritual conditions that must be observed if the exercise of doubt is not to be a dangerous enterprise indeed.

But the Church can also be asked to consider the unavoidable problems that it has had a part in creating. The more it particularizes and dogmatizes, the more it alienates a great portion of humanity. It could avoid this by receiving those who cannot believe wholeheartedly.

We can conceive of a marginal but officially recognized position for such persons. These persons could explain themselves, give obvious proof of their honesty, show good motives for their doubt, and make it understood that they constitute a whole group which claims *its* part in Christian salvation.

2. The Church of John XXIII and Paul VI invites Protestants and all men of good will to join a religious fraternity. At the same time, the new dogmas (Immaculate Concep-

tion, Papal Infallibility, Assumption) are reaffirmed. Those who doubt these dogmas, therefore, should be treated as Christians. Many are uncertain about other dogmas and are, nevertheless, close to Christ.

It is to be hoped that one day an objective debate will take place between unbelievers and theologians. This would lead to clarifications helpful to both parties. On both sides we meet honest men who aspire to a total confrontation, to a strictly objective examination of the problems, who desire a progressive and implacable unveiling of reality. To date, the healthy conditions necessary for such a meeting have been lacking, and this has been a great handicap. There is no reason why we cannot start to work now to create these conditions.

The first step, obviously, is for each side to unconditionally accept what the other has to contribute and to be ready to receive a formerly suspect idea if it turns out to be valid. Then a fruitful debate can begin—and it will continue for a century or more. We should allow it to follow its course, checking our desire for a quick conclusion, granting it the enormous amount of time it will take to mature.

A fruitful debate presupposes that each side adopts a straightforward position. No question should be suppressed or regarded as suspect. No one should be held in contempt for any problems he may have. Then too, they must agree upon a common method; and I, for one, feel that this is possible.

Through exacting questions the unbeliever can lead the Christian to a better understanding of his fundamental certainties, helping him to grasp the relationship of his conclusions to his premises. A theologian should be able to explain why he believes in divine Revelation, point to the evidence which supports this belief, and indicate how his results relate to his conviction that an ineffable richness is to be found in Christianity. And if the unbeliever is not unduly obstinate, he should be able to grasp the legitimate affirmations of his partner. If the unbeliever does not subscribe to certain conclusions, he will state why; possibly he will say that *he has not yet seen enough* of what constitutes the original perfection of Christianity to be able to honestly determine the consequences it entails. He will ask the theologian, "Are you yourself sure that you do not put too much weight on your basic evidence, on material of specific value to a Christianity lived day by day, and that you do not go too far in the conclusions you draw from this?" We will then be brought back to our own problem—to fully comprehend the greatness in Christianity and to understand what it implies.

It is possible for Catholics and unbelievers to have a deep exchange through studying such problems. We should all give it serious thought. It is true that the conditions for such a debate are hard to come by. But if both sides can adopt an attitude of humility and understanding, they can work in common on a project of enormous value, I would even say work *in communion,* in the unity of a completely honest spiritual research. At this juncture, this is only possible in very limited circles. But many of our contemporaries, and notably those who are obliged to live in doubt, can begin preparing the soil, and this in itself will help them to find the path to their own personal progress.

The Roman Catholic Church is necessary—but it needs margins. Why not face realities? These margins will be formed, with or without the Church's consent. It would be a truly great liberation today if the Church were to clearly recognize these margins, to recognize the legitimacy of a suspended adherence subject to certain spiritual conditions.[1]

Salvation must be proposed to everyone, through ways that do not contradict the individual conscience. But, today, the means of salvation which have been considered natural and necessary are inaccessible to a great many people. *A portion of humanity can still be saved with the strictest traditional ecclesiastical methods; but another portion, at least equal in size, cannot be.* This is a broad and general fact, and we must make up our minds to face it.

The Church is not set aside for one category of temperaments. Therefore, we must find other methods. This will be a long process; the Church will not accept new principles without a good deal of caution, and rightfully so. Yet a part of mankind is asking for its rights, especially those people who cannot subscribe to all the assertions of the Church in a sincere manner. They ask to be allowed the only type of faith by which they can hope for salvation: a profound adherence to Christianity which, nevertheless, does not exclude certain doubts.

These people have the faith of suffering, the faith of desire, the faith of adherence to everything that is pure and true. May they not be rejected by the believing community. May they not be thrust into outer darkness. May the Church be merciful to them, and understand the religious value of their need!

NOTES

1. First, that of not distrusting the dogmas, of trying to tap the nourishing essence which they in all likelihood express.